UFO'S

and the
Alien Agenda

UFO'S

and the
Alien Agenda

BOB LARSON

THOMAS NELSON PUBLISHERS
Nashville • Atlanta • London • Vancouver
Printed in the United States of America

Unless otherwise noted, Scripture quotations are from THE NEW KING JAMES VERSION. Copyright © 1979, 1980, 1982, 1990, Thomas Nelson, Inc., Publishers.

Scripture quotations noted KJV are from The King James Version of the Holy Bible.

Larson, Bob, 1944-
  UFOs and the alien agenda : uncovering the mystery behind UFOs and the paranormal / by Bob Larson.
      p. cm.
  Includes bibliographical references.
  ISBN 0-7852-7182-1 (pbk.)
    1. Occultism--Religious aspects--Christianity.   2. Unidentified flying objects--Religious aspects--Christianity. I. Title.
  BR115.03L37   1997
  261.5'13--dc21   97-20782
                                                                          CIP

                    1 2 3 4 5 6 QBP 02 01 00 99 98 97
                  Printed in the United States of America

CONTENTS

PART I

Is Anybody Out There?

CHAPTER ONE

Heaven's Gate or Hell's Door?

For days I had heard about the Hale-Bopp comet. I read newspapers and scanned illustrations of its approximate position in the hours after sunset. I watched television news reports with video clips of its luminescence. Still I had not seen it for myself; I was either too busy to walk outside, or when I did look for it, the sky was too overcast. However, on the evening of Wednesday, March 26, 1997, the skies were clear, and I easily spotted the ball of ice glowing in the northwest sky.

I was awestruck. The streaking sentinel, an ancient chunk of rock twenty-five miles across, lit up the dark emptiness of space. What I beheld had not been witnessed in 4,210 years! I stood alone on my back porch, overwhelmed by this spectacular and yet sublime sight. *Just think,* I said to myself, *what I'm watching was last seen when the Great Pyramid of Giza was young, and the grandeur that would be Rome and Greece was still centuries in the future!*

Hale-Bopp's fuzzy tail glistened against the black void of the universe, putting on a show as the most splendid body in the heavens. I remembered how faint Kohoutek, which was supposed to be the largest comet, seemed in 1973; I also remembered the dire predictions of some prophecy preachers who said the comet was a sign of the End Times and the coming of Christ. And then in 1986, Halley's comet, which had been so very visible seventy years earlier, was also so feeble that few people saw it. But Hale-Bopp's glory was undiminished. The silver extremity of its glowing exhaust trailed for millions of miles.

To the ancients, a comet signaled auspicious circumstances, often heralding the rise and fall of kingdoms. What did star gazers predict when they saw this comet thousands of years ago? Since the sun, moon, and stars were worshiped as gods, they probably thought the divinities were trying to tell earthlings something. But what? Whether the gods were angry or smiling depended on the particular cosmology of the culture.

For instance, today's scientists might gaze on Hale-Bopp as a clue to the origins of the universe, a wandering component of the solar system, supposedly present at the beginning of "creation," some 4.6 billion years ago. But for me, Hale-Bopp was simply a wonder.

Moments after viewing the comet, I turned on the television to catch the late evening news and learned that some saw the comet as a call to death. I watched in shock.

"There were thirty-nine bodies found inside the mansion. All had been dead for several days with no signs of trauma," a representative from the San Diego sheriff's office said solemnly. "They were all dressed alike in dark pants and new tennis shoes. The first detectives to enter noticed a strong odor, and now we're waiting for the hazardous materials team to check things out. It appears to be a mass suicide, having something to do with UFOs."

I went to bed wondering who had committed this unthinkable act and why. The next morning, answers began unfolding.

I logged onto the Internet and found the World Wide Web site that news reports said was related to the tragedy, www.highersource.com. As the words *Higher Source* scrolled across my screen, I read the online advertising for their computer service. The background to the main logo featured stars and galactic imagery, not an uncommon motif for a Website. "We at Higher Source not only cater to customizing Websites that will enhance your company image, but strive to make your transition into the world of cyberspace a very easy and fascinating experience," the homepage read.

TV reporters said this company was the front for some kind of cult whose other Website was called www.heavensgate.com. As I logged on to that homepage, the message *Red Alert* periodically flashed above the horizontal word *HEAVEN'S*, bisected by the vertical word *GATE*. Directly beneath the logo I read: "As promised—the keys to Heaven's Gate are here again in Ti and Do (the UFO two) as they were in Jesus and his Father 2,000 years ago."

Quickly I called my broadcast production staff together. "I'm changing the subject of today's radio program. The new topic is 'Higher Source Suicide,'" I told them.

For the next four hours I downloaded page after page of Heaven's Gate information, which explained a complex mix of esoteric philosophy and metaphysical UFO speculation. By show time, I was ready to reveal what the secular media had ignored—the diabolical hell that was hidden behind the so-called Heaven's Gate!

The Show About the
Heaven's Gate Suicide

I began that day's broadcast as I always did: "Hello, America, welcome to *Talk-Back with Bob Larson.* I'll be here for the next hour, telling you what's on my mind."

Then I cited the grim statistics: Sheriff's deputies had found twenty-one women and eighteen men dead, covered with purple triangular shrouds, inside a cream-colored, 1.6-million-dollar mansion in Rancho Sante Fe, California. They ranged in age from twenty to seventy-two. Most carried identification packets in their shirt pockets, along with little pieces of paper containing a suicide recipe: Take pudding or applesauce and mix it with phenobarbital, drink it down with alcohol, then lie back and relax.

At the foot of each of their beds or cots was a packed suitcase. Every victim had a five-dollar bill and several quarters in a pocket, along with a tube of lip balm. I quoted Dr. Brian Blackbourne, the San Diego County medical examiner who looked soberly into the television camera and said, "It seemed to be a group decision. It was very planned, sort of immaculately carried out."

I explained to the audience that Higher Source was a Web design firm, which earned money for a cult that believed the appearance of the Hale-Bopp comet was a "marker," indicating a mass suicide was necessary to leave this world for "the Next Level."

"Let me point out a few of the in-house words the Heaven's Gate group used to describe their beliefs," I said to my radio audience. "I will add a verbal inflection to my voice [shown here in italics] to distinguish their cult terms. They referred to the human body as a *container,* a *vehicle* that had to be put off before they could graduate from their *classroom.*"

Then I paused. "They were looking for a UFO that would take them to the *Level Above Human,* a place they referred to as *Their World.* In other words, they believed there was an extraterrestrial world inhabited by advanced aliens, and to enter that world they had to go through *Heaven's Gate.* The coming of the Hale-Bopp comet provided a *window* to pass through that gate."

I stopped to take a quick sip of the cold water I always have next to me as I do my show. What I was describing was so bizarre, I wondered if anyone in radioland really understood it. Then I went on.

"Let me read from their literature," I said, hoping a direct quote might make more sense: "'Entering the Kingdom of Heaven, and leaving behind this world, means leaving family, sensuality, selfish desires, your human mind, and even your human body, if it be required of you—all mammalian ways, thinking and behavior. Remember, Jesus was sent for one purpose only, to say, "'If you want to go to Heaven, I can take you through that gate—it requires everything of you.'"'"

Sifting through the stack of pages I had printed from the Internet, I found the piece of paper I wanted to refer to next. Then I continued with another direct quote: "'When we arrive at *Their Kingdom,* we can expect boundless caring and nurturing.'"

My sigh of frustration was audible over the air. I shook my head, still not quite willing to believe what I was reading. I was sad for the families of the victims, but I was also intrigued by what this senseless act said about the spiritual void people are desperately trying to fill.

I laid down the paper and leaned closer to the microphone. In a hushed tone, I addressed a particularly amazing entry on their Website. "You may not believe this," I told my radio listeners, "but this cult has devoted an entire section of their teachings to what they have labeled as 'Our Position Against Suicide!'"

I explained to the audience that cult members compared themselves to the Jews of Masada, who killed themselves in A.D. 73 rather than be tortured or enslaved by the Romans.

"But listen to this twisted way of justifying suicide," I said. "They refer to it as *evacuating* their bodies. In fact, they claim the real suicide is to 'turn against the Next Level when it is being offered.' What they are saying is that you and I, the sane ones left alive on this planet, have committed suicide by not taking advantage of the opportunity to kill ourselves so we can be beamed up to Hale-Bopp's UFO!"

By this time I was certain my audience must be thoroughly confused, so I decided to go to a commercial break to give listeners a chance to review these thoughts before I told them the most outlandish part.

When the announcer's voice and the sound of the segue reintroducing the show played through my earphones, I punched the ON button to reactivate my microphone. Off the cuff I commented, "Who Ti and Do were has not yet been revealed. I wish my new book, *UFOs and the Alien Agenda,* was off the press, because there is a section in it that sounds very similar to what is going on."

Then, without knowing what would be revealed in the next twenty-four hours, I said, "What has happened reminds me of the Bo and Peep cult of the 1970s. There is a consistency between what they taught and what happened in Rancho Sante Fe."

Before going to listeners' calls I needed to cover one more strange aspect of the Heaven's Gate cult—the twisted Christian theology that led to this disaster. "This cult taught that Christ was an *alien* who came to Earth to take over the body of a human called Jesus. An alien *moved into* the body of Jesus at His baptism by John the Baptist," I explained. "Heaven's Gate thought that when the Holy Spirit descended as a dove, it was really an extraterrestrial coming into the *receptacle* of Jesus' body, who was chosen as the *Next Level Representative.*

"Now fasten your spiritual seat belt," I warned the audience. "This part is going to get really strange. The Heaven's Gate cult believed in demons and what they called *negative forces.* Let me quote again directly from them: 'Space alien Luciferians, fallen angels, use discarnate spirits, the minds of those who have died, to program people not to believe in astrology, metaphysics, the paranormal, and UFOs. They do this so they won't be found out. These Luciferian space races are the humans' greatest enemy. They even try to make deals with human governments to permit them (the Luciferians) to engage in biological experimentation (through abductions) in exchange for technically advanced modes of travel.'"

I nearly laughed at how ludicrous all this sounded. This cult had turned conventional Christian theology upside down. They endorsed astrology and other occult practices, which the Bible condemns. And they said that the forces of Lucifer did not want humanity involved in the occult because it was the way to higher alien truth, rather than God's prohibition against indulging in such things because they are a danger to the soul!

Then I quoted the real clincher, which showed the spiritual corruptness of the cult. "Luciferians want society to stay blinded," I read from the Heaven's Gate Internet page. "These fallen angels want people to be married, be good parents, reasonable churchgoers, and graciously accept death with the hope that through His shed blood, or some other equally worthless religious precept, you will go to Heaven after your death. This is Luciferian programming."

The cult's answer to this satanic deception? "If you want to go to Heaven, here is your window," I read further. "That window of opportunity requires an incarnate, human *Representative* (Ti and Do) and those who will go with that Representative will literally leave the human kingdom and Earth. That window of Heaven will not open again until another civilization is planted. The same grace that was available at the end of the first Representative's mission 2,000 years ago is available now with our presence."

Because there was so much to say about Heaven's Gate I only took a couple of callers during the show, but the last one, named Sherry, summed up one of the most important points of the program.

"I have my Bible right in front of me," Sherry said, "and it says in 2 Thessalonians 2:11 that in the End Times, God will allow a strong delusion to take over mankind, so that people will believe a lie, and they will perish because they don't love the truth."

"I agree with you, Sherry," I said.

"I can see how we're being prepared to accept the idea of aliens, with movies like *The Empire Strikes Back*," Sherry continued. "It used to be that you were the crazy one if you believed in aliens. Now, you're the crazy one if you don't."

The next morning, Good Friday, I awoke to newspaper headlines that revealed the identity of the cult's Representative, Do (pronounced *doe*). He was Marshall Herff Applewhite. His "elder member," Ti (pronounced *tee*), was Bonnie Lu Trousdale Nettles.

Ti and Do Uncovered

I had been right the day before. Ti and Do *were* Bo and Peep, the leaders of an earlier version of Heaven's Gate that first surfaced in the 1970s.

Wanting to check what I had said about them, I reached for my soon-to-be published manuscript and turned to this passage in the chapter on UFO cults:

> One of the more bizarre cult followings surrounded the infamous scam of a man and a woman in Oregon who called themselves Bo and Peep. Their real identities were that of Marshall Herff Applewhite, a former opera singer and one-time mental patient, and Bonnie Lu Trousdale Nettles, an astrologer who nursed Applewhite through a mental breakdown. Bonnie's credentials also included credit card theft and the alleged ability to contact a European monk who died several centuries ago. Bo and Peep called their cult Human Individual Metamorphosis, and they claimed only a few selected humanoids would qualify for a UFO ride to happiness on another planet.
>
> The two charmed hundreds to follow them on their parapsychological journeys as they spun tales of a spacecraft hovering somewhere over Nebraska, waiting to transport true believers into an upper vibrational level, known to Christians as heaven. They promised that a UFO would transport them directly to the kingdom of Jesus Christ. Many converts abandoned everything they owned for this journey and headed for collection points where they fervently believed they would be visited by aliens from outer space to whisk them away to a galactic paradise.

Bo and Peep described themselves as "space fetuses," and their ideology read like a garbled mixture of Bible misinterpretation and a bad *Star Trek* plot. To qualify for the extraterrestrial hope, abduction candidates had to go through an "overcoming process," which meant signing over all worldly assets as a way of breaking the bonds of Earth. By the time the fraud was exposed, hundreds of people had left family and friends to seek a window on the kingdom of God, which supposedly opens once every two thousand years.

Reading the last line of what I had written about the cult several weeks earlier sent a chill up my spine. My words were almost prophetic. At the time I had penned the original Bo and Peep entry to this book, some fifteen hundred miles away in San Diego County, California, Marshall Applewhite was already instructing his followers in the final stages of the worst mass suicide on American soil. The "window" they were seeking was supposedly found behind a massive boulder of ice, hurtling through space at forty thousand miles per hour.

From my old research files I pulled out several articles about UFOs; the material had been stashed away in folders for twenty-two years. Two of the most interesting pieces were a *Time* magazine story, dated October 20, 1975, and a *Newsweek* article with the same cover date.

The *Time* headline declared, "Out of This World." "Eyewitnesses describe Bo and Peep ('the two') as being in their 40s and having glassy, hollow-looking eyes," the magazine said. "The Two expect to be assassinated sometime soon, rise from the dead in 3 1/2 days, and then leave for home in a UFO."[1]

Newsweek had this to say, in a piece titled "Bo-Peep's

Flock": "Led by a look-alike, dress-alike, middle-aged couple, this latest band of zealots has persuaded people to leave possessions, homes and even children behind and follow them somewhere into the parapsychological wilderness. So far they have committed nothing more insidious than an assault on credibility."[2]

If only that assessment had remained true!

MORE ABOUT BO AND PEEP

As incisive as my words in the manuscript were, thousands of reporters all across the nation were digging deeper into this national tragedy and coming up with more strange facts about "the two." The tale they uncovered about the UFO-obsessed "Bonnie and Clyde" was more peculiar than any fictional saga. The cult's uniform buzz cuts and gender-neutral clothing, which would usher them into some kind of androgynous paradise in space, were just a few of the unbelievable ideas fostered by the former nurse and the ex-choirmaster.

Marshall Herff Applewhite was born the son of an austere Presbyterian minister. The young Applewhite also considered the ministry, and even entered seminary. He was a talented singer and instrumentalist who ended up teaching music at the Catholic University of St. Thomas, in Houston, Texas. On the side he led choirs at Episcopalian and Unitarian churches, and sang with the Houston Grand Opera. And, according to credible reports, he privately used drugs and became sexually involved with another male at the university, leading to his dismissal.

In the early 1970s Applewhite's private torment over his confused sexuality led him to check into a psychiatric hospital. He told his sister, Louise Winant, that he was suffering from a heart blockage to disguise his true intentions: to find a cure for his homosexuality.

In this hospital he met his soul mate, Bonnie Lu Nettles, a nurse who convinced him they had known each other in past lives. Nettles and Applewhite concocted a weird dogma that in order to rise to the next evolutionary level of human consciousness and be worthy of the attention of advanced aliens, true disciples of the Kingdom of Heaven had to give up the use of their sexual organs. Years later, Applewhite even underwent surgical castration, and convinced at least six of his suicidal male followers to also undergo the procedure.

The secular media covering this story have almost universally suggested that the horror of Heaven's Gate would not have happened if Applewhite had accepted his homosexuality. Conservative Christians, who believe that homosexual behavior is unacceptable, argue that his indulgence in this behavior was a moral violation that clouded his spiritual judgment, thus leading to other reprehensible deeds.

Applewhite's struggles with his homosexuality and bisexuality eventually caused him to declare that reproduction was actually evil. "It's barbaric, it's beneath me," he boldly proclaimed.[3] He taught followers that it would be better to follow the ideal of the alien Kingdom Representatives, who made human beings by implanting bodies with minds and then later dropped souls into them once they had matured.

By the time Applewhite left the psychiatric hospital he was hearing voices. Nettles, who had dabbled in various occult and New Age disciplines, left her husband to join her Bo on a hippie-like nomadic journey across the western U.S. Along the way they became convinced they were the two witnesses the apostle John spoke of in Revelation, chapter eleven, and that flying saucers would be the way out of the coming apocalypse. They started recruiting followers. Their chaotic lifestyles took on more order and purpose when one disciple turned over an insurance settlement of about $300,000 to the two.

Even with this windfall, however, their disciples still begged for money and food. Wherever they went, they lived by what they called "God's law," and consequently left behind a string of unpaid gas and motel bills. At one point, Bo and Peep were thrown in jail for using stolen credit cards. Eventually they took new names from the top of the musical scale—Ti and Do—and headed for the New Mexico mountains outside of Albuquerque.

During this sojourn they began telling devotees that the Earth was about to be recycled and an evacuation was in order for those who were worthy of the Kingdom of God. The passport to this extraterrestrial paradise was a sense of community based on exacting rituals. Members sometimes wore hoods over their heads, and their chores were altered every twelve minutes, in accordance with messages sent by Do's command via beepers. Everyone was given a "check partner" to ensure there would be no backsliding or contrary thinking.

The cult's attempt to forge a lifestyle devoid of sensory pleasure and sexual gratification allowed an extreme form of asceticism to emerge. By denying their sexual and sensory identities, members of the cult became more like the first-century Gnostics, who believed that the body was evil and the enemy of true mystical enlightenment. The *gnosis* (Greek for *knowledge*—usually referring to a secret body of truth) preached by Applewhite also saw the body as an earthbound prison that needed to be shed.

Their eccentric piety caused them to be so self-absorbed that they never spoke to outsiders about their faith in the aliens who guided their lives so meticulously. En route to their starry utopia, they practiced a regimen of eating the same food at the same hours. Their shapeless clothes and identical wedding bands (they considered themselves all married to each other) were a symbol of their asexual commitment to the group-self.

Then, in the summer of 1996, Do moved the entire clan to Rancho Sante Fe, California, and rented the spacious home where the mass suicide took place. They chose this particular house because they thought it looked like a spaceship.

In the months that followed, they ensconced themselves inside the mansion, preparing for the end and operating the Higher Source Website design company. In their final days they ate at the local Pancake House and began videotaping their farewells, giddily describing their joy over their coming deaths. As one of the castrated men put it, "It's just the happiest day of my life."

When I saw that tape I wondered, *How could anyone view suicide in that way?* Yet the spiritual roots for this ultimate act of "sacred" devotion were present all along. In fact, a close look at what Heaven's Gate believed might lead one to say that it's amazing they did not attempt a dramatic act sooner.

Five Factors Set the Stage

Five factors clearly set the stage for these cult suicides.

I. APOCALYPTIC ERROR

Ti and Do claimed to be space-age shepherds of God (hence the names Bo and Peep), the Almighty's two witnesses, as described in Revelation 11:3–12. The pair suggested they would also be assassinated, just like the prophets of John's Apocalypse. Then they would rise again three and one-half days later, to be beamed heavenward to a waiting UFO. In the mid-1970s, the two referred to their murder and ascension as "the Demonstration."

As far back as 1976 Bo confidently declared, "While we have no desire to escape the Demonstration, neither are we people who find pleasure in being killed. The world does not have to choose to do us in, but the chances that it won't happen are about as great as that a rain will wash all the red dirt out of Oklahoma."[4]

That the followers of Do would believe such a garbled interpretation of Scripture shows their shallow understanding of what the Bible actually teaches. Several glaring inconsistencies between the biblical requirements in Revelation 11:5–6 for the two witnesses and Ti and Do make this obvious. These false "shepherds" did not devour their enemies with fire from their mouths (v. 5), they did not cause rain to quit falling (v. 6), and they did not turn waters to blood (v. 6).

The witnesses of the Revelation were already in heaven when Zechariah prophesied their coming (Zech. 4:11–14) at least five hundred years before Christ! Since it is appointed unto men once to die (Heb. 9:27), it can be determined that Enoch and Elijah of the Old Testament, who were both taken directly into heaven without dying, are the only two reasonable candidates.

Like many end-time cults, the Heaven's Gate group obscured their intent under the guise of urgent spirituality. For various, and often self-centered reasons, millennial sects seek to accelerate the coming of Armageddon, a kind of infantile apocalypse. To such groups, death is not an enemy but the gateway to life itself. With a mixture of paranoia and passion, they envision a better world waiting, so why hang around here?

Applewhite's disenchantment with his own neutered body, and his fear of losing followers, may have led him to hasten the union with extraterrestrials he had long pledged to produce. In contrast, evangelical Christians, who share some of the same concerns about the end of this age, generally heed the command of Christ to "occupy" until he returns (Luke 19:13 KJV). They are content to prayerfully await the day and the hour that only the Father in heaven knows.

2. THE ECLECTIC CONNECTION

Applewhite's religious interests ran the gamut of the paranormal: from astrology to past-lives regression, from reincarnation to spirit communication. He rejected Christian orthodoxy, and in its place melded together a spiritually perilous mixture of parapsychological and mystical beliefs. This eclecticism allowed him to borrow from a variety of occult traditions.

From the Mormons he got the idea of ascendancy to godhood and the doctrine that all human beings begin life as the spirit children of heavenly parents. From Eastern religions he borrowed the vision of reincarnating cycles of life, which ascend on an evolutionary path. From Scientology he co-opted the concept of humans having once been god-like aliens, or thetans as they are known in *Dianetics.*

And from apocalyptic millennialism he took the eccentric belief that a small group of true believers would be saved from global disaster. The exact number to meet their demise came from another occult discipline, numerology: thirty-nine committed suicide because that is a sacred number (three plus nine equals twelve, the number of Christ's disciples).

This cosmology needed constant adjustment, however, as Applewhite's various promises of alien encounters failed to materialize. Instructions on when and where to meet the next spaceship were often contradictory, so having a religious potpourri allowed an expanding revelation of truth, which kept Ti and Do's followers preoccupied.

3. THE NEW AGE INFLUENCE

Applewhite and Nettles were both deeply involved in alternative religious movements and even started a New Age bookstore. Bo declared his first attraction to Peep was when she read his horoscope. For her part, Nettles consulted the advice of spiritualists, who foretold that an important man would be coming into her life. In Houston, Applewhite and Nettles opened a Christian Arts Center, specializing in Theosophy, astrology, mysticism, and healing. They began communicating with what they said were space beings, who urged them to abandon all worldly pursuits. This New Age occultism, with its morally murky approach to defining values, provided the subjective environment that nurtured Applewhite's UFO fantasies.

The selfishness found in the New Age idea of "finding your own truth" and the egoistical search for one's "higher self" reached its epitome with Heaven's Gate. Applewhite's crew opted out of the coming conflagration by leaving six billion people behind while saving their own celestial necks.

Just as those who wear crystals to enhance spirituality or sit under plastic pyramids to consume cosmic vibrations, the computer nerds of the Rancho Santa Fe mansion cared nothing for their fellow man. "Follow me," was all Applewhite said, as he invited those who saw his videos to join the forthcoming assisted suicide journey. Feeding the hungry or sheltering the homeless was not their idea of religion. "Beam me up, Marshall," was.

4. ABANDONMENT OF THE BIBLE

The strange contortion that Heaven's Gate put on Christian teaching made for a combustible theological mixture.

Applewhite's reverse psychology—claiming that Satan wanted to keep humanity from indulging in the occult—made his followers susceptible to absurd metaphysical teaching. They walked open-eyed into the arms of evil supernatural forces, while thinking they were doing God's will. Twisting logic this way led to other deceptions, such as redefining suicide. Many cults thrive because they explain the inexplicable by such odd leaps of argumentation.

Cult members seldom questioned this Luciferian logic, because it came from "divine revelation," channeled through what Bo and Peep called a "chain of mind." The only valid information about UFOs and any accompanying cosmology was that which flowed in a direct line from the Father to the Two. Thus, the roles of Applewhite and Nettles were solidified and made them the only intermediaries between the Next Level and human consciousness.

Cult members did read the Bible constantly, but it was a special red-underlined edition. They obviously ignored the warning of Matthew 24:24, "For false christs and false prophets will rise and show great signs and wonders to deceive, if possible, even the elect."

In fact, Do declared, "My being here now is actually a continuation of that last task as it was promised to those who were [Jesus'] students 2,000 years ago." When Ti died in 1985, Do said that she was really "My Father" in heaven, in this way supplanting at least two of the Holy Trinity.

5. SCIENTIFIC IGNORANCE AND INTELLECTUAL ILLITERACY

Members of the cult accepted the teachings of Applewhite without any logical challenge from a scientific standpoint. Objective thought processes were pointless. There was no need to ponder any serious existential questions. The universe was divided into two uncomplicated camps: the thirty-eight faithful followers of Do against a corrupt system of religious institutions under the control of Lucifer, whom Do called "Lucy." Heaven's Gate disciples contemplated nothing more profound than rising at four o'clock every morning to gaze into the sky and long for their true home somewhere in the heavens.

Known scientific information about the Hale-Bopp comet was ignored in favor of an irrational assumption based on sci-fi conjecture and pure superstition. In one videotaped utterance, Applewhite assured his followers, "If the extent of your religious background was *Star Trek,* that in itself could be the best background you could have, if you could accept this as truth, if you could accept this as reality."

What kind of power caused people to ignore all reason and scientific data? Joan Culpepper, an early disciple, gave an interesting insight. "An extraordinary thing happened when I was listening to Bo," she explained. "It was as if a strong force came down over my mind and shut off my critical sense. I think the Two have strong psychic powers and the ability to brainwash people."[5]

Devotion to the cult's goals was so overwhelming, in fact, that a videotaped message by one of those who committed suicide contained this unswerving assessment: "I am looking forward to this. I am nothing without Ti and Do."

How could people be so deluded? Could others make the same mistake? Could Heaven's Gate happen again?

Will Heaven's Gate Happen Again?

The spiritual marketplace available to America at the end of this millennium offers a dangerous mixture of exotic ideas, any one of which could spark the fuse leading to another

Heaven's Gate horror. Like the Athenians, whom the apostle Paul described as "very religious" (Acts 17:22), the United States is a religious hothouse. An aspiring, charismatic, spiritual leader like Marshall Applewhite can garner a flock quickly by promising ultimate meaning to those seeking to fill a spiritual void in their lives.

Perhaps a hundred or more UFO groups like Heaven's Gate, with an interest in pursuing flying saucers, operate openly or clandestinely. Generally, UFO devotees say they are not religious but "spiritual," a designation that could range from an interest in talking to plants to waiting to board the mother ship. Leaders of these cults offer esoteric truth, hidden spiritual insight which is available only to initiates. These seekers of occult knowledge are potentially vulnerable to an exploitative cult leader who offers instant karma when the next spaceship arrives.

The social dynamics of Applewhite's manipulation of his followers have been practiced by many other modern cults. Whether he deliberately borrowed these techniques is not known, but the result is the same: a homogeneous band of zealous disciples willing to die for his ideas. The dynamic that helped Do achieve this was relational isolation.

RELATIONAL ISOLATION

Most family members of the victims declared they had not seen their loved ones in years and had no contact with them during the time the cult wandered about the country. Early in the cult's history, Applewhite taught that "the need for affection at any level, the need to be with someone, the need to be alone are all stumbling blocks. To make it to the Next Level they must give up all their addictions."

Even their own children? "Children are not eligible for the space flight because the decision to go must be made by each individual, and youngsters are not capable of making such a momentous choice," Do explained.[6]

Cult members who were parents gave away their children, spouses forsook their mates, and adult children refused to speak with their parents. This emotionally incestuous isolation separated the cult members from all outside critical inquiry. It also voided all external reality in favor of the internal illusions of the cult. This detachment made whatever Applewhite taught loom large in the minds of cult members and negated any opinions to the contrary. Such isolation was crucial to the cult's success, since investigations into the lives of those who followed Do shows that they were disconcertingly ordinary people. Thus, extraordinary measures were necessary to maintain their devotion.

Each member's name was changed to demonstrate the futility of individual identities. No contact with the outside world through watching television or listening to the radio was allowed. An employee of a firm for which Higher Source (the cult's computer company) designed Web pages observed that cult members never permitted anyone to shake their hands or touch them in any way. Above all, parental contact was off-limits, because Do claimed that family members had the ability to draw cult members away by tugging at them from "vibrational levels."

The potential for duplicating Do's achievement is very real. Already existing UFO cults or new cults could mimic Applewhite's gate to heaven, adding their own twists to his cosmology. And former cult members say that surviving disciples of Do, known as the "ground crew," are still seeking to rendezvous with their translated leader. Some still frequent New Age energy centers in the Southwest, hoping to meet up with a reincarnated Applewhite. They believe he will either come to them in another "vehicle" (body) or swoop down from the skies in a spaceship to pick them up.

And at least one copycat "evacuation" has already occurred. Robert Louis Nichols of Marysville, California, made a belated attempt to join the Heaven's Gate crew by committing suicide, leaving behind a note expressing his desire for union with them. "I'm going on the spaceship with Hale-Bopp to be with those who have gone before me," Nichols wrote.[7]

There may never again be a time as ripe as this—when the vernal equinox, a partial lunar eclipse, and a comet all converged. But according to disaffected past members of Heaven's Gate, thousands passed through their ranks and hundreds still secretly believe in what Applewhite taught. All it will take for the next victim is a willingness to suspend disbelief and a desire to accelerate the Second Coming. Given the large number of people with unsatisfied spiritual longings, the conditions may be right, at any moment, for thousands more to enter Heaven's Gate. The ultimate query remains: Will they sail through the gateway to heaven, as the cult promised; or will they find themselves trapped on the doorstep of hell?

Questions Applewhite Never Answered

Marshall Herff Applewhite professed to have the answers his followers were seeking. Yet his early exit from life meant that Do never had to deal with the most pressing questions raised by his ideology.

Can the Darwinian hypothesis be trusted to suggest that somewhere in the vastness of space other intelligent species evolved?

What forms might such aliens take, and would they desire to visit Earth to initiate human contact?

Are unidentified objects in the skies the prelude to a decisive spiritual confrontation signaling the end of time?

Is it possible that the entire UFO controversy is a spiritual phenomenon, rather than a material occurrence, precipitated by malevolent spirit beings?

If we can determine who is really out there, can we also know why they are here, and uncover their true agenda?

These questions are the concern of this book. But first let's look back to the very beginning of the UFO phenomenon in the United States, when Ken Arnold spotted an unidentified flying object outside his aircraft on June 24, 1947.

CHAPTER TWO

The Alien Invasion

As a child growing up on a Nebraska farm in the fifties, I was fascinated by unidentified flying objects, like the ones Ken Arnold spotted in 1947. Every kid in America knew the story. Arnold, a thirty-two-year-old Boise, Idaho, businessman and veteran air rescue pilot, was flying his single-engine, private plane in the vicinity of Mount Rainier, Washington. At an elevation of about 9,200 feet, just a few minutes before three o'clock on a sunny afternoon, a blue-white flash exploded in front of him.

Stunned, Arnold looked out the cockpit in every direction. Nothing could be seen, except a DC-4 airplane far to his rear. Arnold dismissed what happened and settled back. Then a second flash momentarily blinded him. This time he could see the light ahead of his plane. As he strained to focus on it, Arnold deciphered a configuration of dazzling objects skimming the mountaintops. Because of the speed they were flying, Arnold assumed they were part of a squadron of new air force fighter jets. But the more he looked at the phenomenon, the less it looked like conventional aircraft.

As best he could gauge, the objects were about twenty miles away, nine of them flying in tight formation. He noticed that the blinding flash of light was created by the blaze of sunlight that reflected from their mirror-like surfaces as they dipped and banked. Arnold thought they looked to have wingspans of about fifty feet. He decided to measure their speed by calculating the time lapse as they passed by one mountaintop and sped toward another. The formation shot beyond Mount Rainier and then zipped over the crest of Mount Adams in one minute, forty-two seconds. Arnold reached for his air map. The peaks were forty-seven miles apart. That meant an air speed of 1,656 miles per hour, three times faster than any existing jet!

An hour later, Arnold landed at Yakima and told his friends on the ground what he had seen. "Rockets," one of them said. But rockets don't bank in flight. "Experimental jets," another suggested. But no one knew of any military facility that would be using this area. Besides, experimental craft fly solitary missions, not in formation and usually not in areas frequented by commercial flights, such as the Seattle-San Francisco flight path, which these objects crossed.

After an intense discussion, Arnold took off for Pendleton, Oregon. By the time he got there news of his experience had intrigued a group of reporters. Surrounding his plane, they barraged him with questions about his experience and were impressed with his factual verification. He had flown more than four thousand hours and knew the Cascade Mountains area well. The reporters pressed for some verbal description of what Arnold had seen. He reflected and then suggested the flying objects were a little like speedboats in rough water, or maybe like the tail of a kite. Then he uttered the words that have since defined the UFO phenomenon. In an off-the-cuff fashion Ken Arnold declared that the mysterious objects flew "like a saucer would if you skipped it across the water."

From that description, newspaper headline writers coined the term *flying saucers*. Five decades later, the name still sticks, though the descriptions of unidentified flying objects (UFOs) seem to have grown more sophisticated with each passing year and each successive *Star Trek* movie sequel. Feared and laughed about, the subject of horror films and scholarly books, UFOs and the mystery surrounding them have survived every attempt at dismissal or documentation.

Ken Arnold's sighting occurred at an opportune time in the national psyche. The late 1940s and early 1950s were years ripe for fear of an alien invasion. Senator Joe McCarthy was hunting for enemies in our midst. Civil defense teams were building bomb shelters in schoolyards. Then the Soviets launched *Sputnik*, their "eye in the sky," the first space vehicle to orbit the Earth. Given that milieu, many Americans feared that the next bright light in the sky might be ushering in visitors from another planet.

Such speculation was partially prompted by an even earlier event: Orson Welles's infamous melodrama, "The War of the Worlds." As a successful actor and radio personality in the 1930s, Welles narrated the *March of Times* radio program and played the part of Lamont Cranston in *The Shadow* mystery series. In 1938, he and his Mercury Players undertook a series of radio dramas adapted from famous fictional works. Simulating a news broadcast, they performed a program based on a novel by Englishman Herbert George Wells. H. G. Wells was a journalist, sociologist, and historian known for his science fiction books such as *The Time Machine* and *The Invisible Man*. In *The War of the Worlds* Wells described Martians, who possessed great intelligence—which necessitated their having "big brains" encased in "big, shapely skulls"—landing on Earth.

I never heard the original account of "The War of the Worlds." That bogus broadcast was before my time. I did read stories about the panic that ensued in the New Jersey countryside when Welles declared that Martians had landed, and it made me curious to see a flying saucer. Nearly every farmer in our county said he had spotted one. They told tales of lights glowing in the sky and strange objects floating in the air and then darting about with incredible speed and maneuverability.

I suppose if I had grown up in the shadow of Wrigley Field or with the Empire State Building in view, the idea of UFOs appearing would have seemed more remote. But out on the prairie, where no ambient light intruded and nighttime solitude was easier to come by, the idea of aliens was always a glance-in-the-night away. Then, one night, I saw one. Or thought I did.

MY JUVENILE CLOSE ENCOUNTER

It was a sticky summer evening. The buzz of heat bugs drowned out all other sounds. I stood on the front porch, watching swarms of fireflies in their dazzling display of pyrotechnics. Then it appeared, just across the road and a section's distance of farmland away. It drifted across the eastern horizon, just above the Kotchswars' barn.

The dim light of dusk prevented me from making a positive identification, but my childhood imagination filled in the blanks. "They" were up there in that thing, peering down on me! I was sure their telescopes were studying my every move. I cautiously stepped off the porch into the front yard for a closer look. Dodging a cloud of gnats, I crept across the lawn. Slowly I moved in the direction of the object. It did not seem to be going anywhere in particular, and I could not see the lights that people identified with such spaceships. Gradually the object dimmed from view and melted into the darkening sky.

I never told my parents. Why should I? They wouldn't believe me anyway. Besides, this was an experience too awesome to share with anyone. I figured if I told anyone they would say I had seen an airplane, but I knew better. No question about it, I had seen a flying saucer.

All night I tossed in my bed, wondering if I would ever see it again. Old *Buck Rogers* movie images mingled in my mind with drawings of space aliens I had seen in magazines. I kept the covers pulled over my head as my imagination ran wild. Any moment I expected a blinding light to illuminate our house like the playing field of a Friday night football game. Then I would hear the sound of a roaring engine as the flying saucer returned for a closer look. I was frightened of the possibility, but intrigued by the idea that our little farm was important enough to warrant the attention of visitors from outer space. With all the places they could have checked out, why us?

The aliens in my dreams were frightening creatures with three narrow eyes and antennae sprouting from oversized, bulbous heads. Their skin was scale-like and their fingers resembled long claws. They walked bowlegged, sort of shifting from side to side. Except for a few unintelligible grunts, they said nothing. These hideous beings stalked me, poked me, and gazed at me with evil curiosity.

After an entire night of evading these extraterrestrials, my fear of what I had seen was out of hand. And apparently I was not the only one. Early that next morning the radio station reported that several people had seen something strange in the sky. A government spokesman tried to calm everyone by explaining that a stray weather balloon had wandered over our part of the state. There was no need to worry. No war of the worlds would be fought in a high-plains cornfield.

Call it undaunted childhood inquisitiveness if you wish, but I was undeterred. Weather balloon? No way. It was too flat, too much like a saucer. And it did not drift slowly across the sky. It skipped first one direction, then another, just like Ken Arnold said. President Dwight D. Eisenhower himself could have told me it was not a UFO, and I still would have believed I had seen a spacecraft from another world.

My certainty back then, however, was nothing compared to the current conviction of UFO chasers like Robert Bigelow. He not only believes that extraterrestrials are out there, wanting to communicate with us down here, he has bet the farm on it. In fact, he *bought* the farm.

BIGELOW'S BUNGALOW

Bigelow is a Las Vegas multimillionaire whose fervor regarding UFOs is so strong he plunked down $200,000 for a single plot of land said to be a landing site for saucers. The 480-acre parcel, in the heart of Utah's Uinta Basin, was owned by the Terry Sherman family. For years the Shermans remained silent about their close encounters with UFOs. But once they broke their silence, Bigelow barged in.

The Shermans had seen lights emerging from what they described as circular "doorways," which seemed to appear in midair. Terry Sherman claimed that three cows had been mutilated after one such visitation. Other cows just disappeared. Where the strange craft had been sighted, there were impressions in the soil and circles of flattened grass.

Bigelow, a prominent financier of paranormal investigations, was convinced the tales were true. So he bought out the

Shermans, who were only too happy to move to another ranch down the road. If Bigelow wanted to examine whatever was stealing cows on their property, so be it. Eighteen months of extraterrestrial harassment were enough for them. In fact, the Shermans say, they could have sold the land for much more. Why not wait for a better offer? They did not want to risk running afoul of the spaceships.

Near the reputed UFO landing site, Bigelow has erected an observation building and staffed it with a pair of scientists and a veterinarian. Twenty-four hours a day the staff monitors the land for any unusual occurrences. The pseudoscientific outfit that oversees this operation, called the National Institute for Discovery Science, is also underwritten by Bigelow.

Whatever the institute finds will be published in scientific journals and on the institute's Website. Until then, all aspects of the research are under wraps. Even the Shermans aren't talking. They signed a nondisclosure agreement and are still maintaining the ranch they sold to Bigelow, while living a safe fifteen miles away.[1]

Is it unusual for a UFO enthusiast like Bigelow to go to such lengths to investigate sightings? Not really. Such seriousness about investigating UFO accounts is due both to the number of reports and to the consistency of the observers' stories.

Striking Similarities

Though UFOs have appeared at random times and in different locations, certain details of flying saucer stories are common. Observers usually describe the craft as circular, cylindrical, or spherical in shape, with flashing lights and luminous brilliance. The UFOs often hover near power lines. They may float over a large body of water or near a military installation. Eyewitnesses say the objects change color and shape, appear and disappear, and seemingly defy all known laws of physics.

In just a few seconds UFOs can accelerate from a standing position to speeds clocked at several thousand miles per hour. They often make ninety-degree turns in midair. Left in their wake are vile odors, charred landing spots, and various kinds of electrical interference. UFOs also attract a host of true believers whose tenacious telling of alien sightings has kept the UFO controversy alive. Are such similar stories all the result of overactive imaginations?

Back in Nebraska the farm folks still talk of seeing strange objects in the air. Like the Shermans, their stories are often laced with anecdotes about butchered animals. As far as I know, no Cornhusker has yet admitted to being abducted for sexual experimentation by aliens. The prairie social code would not look favorably on such erotic accounts. But sooner or later some slit-eyed, amorphous monster will do the job, and some poor farmer will live to tell the tale. Then Bigelow will have another farm to buy.

Before you lay down this book because you are too logically minded to swallow fables about three-feet-tall, bald-headed beings with mutated body parts, consider the UFO reports that are not so easy to dismiss. There have been documented accounts of treetops being torn off in the former Soviet Union and an entire forest of thousands of acres being razed. And not all the reports are from kooks. Former president Jimmy Carter said he saw a UFO. So did Ronald Reagan, and so have a host of other responsible citizens.

Perhaps the most important question is this: Who is piloting these craft? Early flying saucer speculation focused on the Russians, in light of their early successes in space exploration. During the cold war fervor of the fifties, everyone assumed the Soviets had a superior technological advantage, even though they couldn't build an automobile anyone wanted. Now, from the perspective of the Evil Empire's collapse, it's obvious they were lucky to get Yury Gagarin, the first man to go into space, off the ground. "Boris" and his buddies were too intent on misleading American military experts into thinking the Soviets had a missile advantage to send antigravity craft halfway around the world just to cut up some cows.

Is our own government concealing the truth? That has always been a popular theory. Almost every movie about UFOs regurgitates that idea with the enthusiasm of an Oliver Stone conspiracy. And every devotee of the Big Cover-Up knows exactly where the secret headquarters is located: Area 51, near Groom Lake, Nevada.

THE AREA 51 FANTASY

Rachel, Nevada, is one of those nice-place-to-visit-but-I-wouldn't-want-to-live-there locations. Even then it's only nice if you're convinced that E. T. really wanted to phone home, and Rachel was the closest place with an intergalactic telephone.

Yet this tiny blink of a town has become a Mecca for the sci-fi faithful. It is the anchor for Nevada's biggest tourist attraction outside of Vegas and Reno: an Extraterrestrial Highway, a ninety-two-mile desolate stretch of road known as State Route 375. It also boasts a watering hole called the Little Ale-Inn. Area 51 certainly does not seem like an extraterrestrial destination; the topography is barren with only an occasional scrub brush or juniper tree punctuating the horizon. Rachel consists of little more than a cluster of mobile homes housing its one hundred citizens. But residents insist this isolation makes the locality the perfect place for alien landings and clandestine government experiments.

Legend has it that a UFO crashed near Roswell, New Mexico, on July 2, 1947. The pieces of the spacecraft and the remains of the aliens who died in the crash were supposedly taken to a secret military installation just over the mountains from Rachel, Nevada. That location is known as Area 51, or Groom Lake, the site of a purported top-secret government base.

What did happen that hot July day fifty years ago? Roswell area citizens of the time said they saw a large glowing object, flying at high speeds, about 10:00 A.M. That night a rancher near Roswell also heard an explosion, so loud that it drowned out the claps of a thunderstorm. Next morning he found fragments of a foil-like substance scattered over a quarter-mile of ground. Supposedly the rancher also turned over a disk-shaped object to an army intelligence officer.

After several days of conflicting reports, Brigadier General Roger Ramey of the Eighth Air Force Headquarters in Fort Worth, Texas, declared the cryptic object was the wreckage of a weather device. He called a press conference and allowed photographers to take a few shots of an unidentifiable shiny substance. Eventually documents surfaced alleging that officials recovered the bodies of four aliens from the Roswell wreckage and kept them from public view.

The Roswell incident spawned a series of other alien tales. Years after the Roswell rancher found the foil, a civil engineer named Barney Barnett came forward, saying that the day after the crash he and some archaeological students found the wreckage of another craft about 250 miles away. The thirty-foot-wide oval spaceship had broken open and spilled bodies across the desert floor in a grisly death scene. The beings were hairless, with tiny eyes and huge heads, wearing one-piece gray coveralls with no zippers. After Barnett's death, friends embellished the story, saying a detail of soldiers had arrived, cordoned off the area, and told everyone to keep quiet about what they had seen.

The rumor of a colossal cover-up at Area 51 has been fed by the military's use of the area for testing exotic aircraft, including the high-flying U-2 and the Stealth fighter. For its part, the government has refused to acknowledge the existence of a base in this area north of Las Vegas, though the area is heavily guarded. Yet something must be going on at Groom Lake, or why would armed security keep gawkers at least seven miles away? Even from that distance, however, the curious have seen mysterious lights and heard deafening roars sweep across the remote terrain. The few civilians who work there are closemouthed, even, according to one Rachel resident, when they're "pretty drunk."[2]

What is in the hangars at Groom Lake? What kind of craft land on the 30,000-foot runway of Area 51? Perhaps the site is nothing more than a testing spot for experimental aircraft. Perhaps no formaldehyde-preserved remains of aliens are behind the barbed wire and secured buildings. For now, it's left to Hollywood, à la *Independence Day,* to speculate about what research may be ongoing and what mysteries are yet unsolved. Until a flying saucer lands somewhere on Earth and someone actually documents that, Rachel, Nevada, will continue to be the focus of UFO conspiracy enthusiasts. And this small burg will continue to lay claim to bordering "the loneliest road in America."[3]

Here, There, and Everywhere

You might think the UFO craze is a relatively recent outgrowth of interest in science fiction. Unquestionably, movies and contemporary literature have encouraged the concept of technologically advanced worlds and travel in outer space. But strange sights appeared in the skies long before our modern era of space flight—or manned flight of any kind—was possible. As might be expected, the visions of unidentified flying objects in each era took on the identities of the worldview of those who saw them.

What has been common to all sightings of peculiar objects in the sky is the notion that there is more to existence than what we observe on Earth. Humanity has been gripped by the suggestion that we are not alone among the myriad of stars.

Throughout the past, reported sightings of curious things in the sky have occurred intermittently. Scientists say that the cave dwellers of 10,000 B.C., who occupied what is now France and Spain, painted subterranean renderings of what we would call UFOs. These "spaceships" were drawn with astounding realism, next to the depictions of bison and horses. A venerable Chinese tale describes a far-off land of flying carts inhabited by one-armed, three-eyed people riding winged chariots.

UFOS IN THE BIBLE?

Some advocates of UFOs claim the Bible validates the concept of unidentified flying objects and visitors from outer space. The Old Testament prophet Elijah ascended into the sky on a "chariot of fire," which appeared "with horses of fire" (2 Kings 2:11). "What better way to depict a rocket ship?" ufologists argue. They also point to Jacob's ladder, which "was set up on the earth, and its top reached to heaven; and there the angels of God were ascending and descending on it" (Gen. 28:12). Surely, they speculate, this was an ancient way to describe a space vehicle and its disembarking extraterrestrial beings.

Other supposed biblical examples of UFOs include the account of Moses leading the Israelites out of Egypt and across Sinai to the Promised Land. When Moses wrote of "a pillar of cloud" by day and a "pillar of fire" by night (Ex. 13:21), was he actually recounting a UFO whose exhaust formed a daytime cloud and was seen as a nighttime fire? Did the power of this exhaust part the Red Sea?

The biblical account that most interests ufologists comes from the prophet Ezekiel, in the first chapter of his book. In about 600 B.C., when Ezekiel was thirty years of age, he had a vision of a tornado-like storm that swept toward him. As he looked closely, the form of four humanoid-type creatures appeared out of the swirling windstorm. He described the commotion as "a great cloud with raging fire engulfing itself; and brightness was all around it and radiating out of its midst like the color of amber, out of the midst of the fire" (v. 4).

Each creature seemed to pilot a brightly glowing, round, flat-shaped object that darted back and forth from one location to another, faster than the eye could follow. Ezekiel interpreted this wheels-within-wheels phenomenon as emanating from "the glory of the LORD" (v. 28). Modern skeptics of Scripture are not so sure of that conclusion.

In 1968 author Erich von Däniken shocked religious sensibilities with his book *Chariots of the Gods?* This bestseller popularized the belief that visitors from outer space mated with human ancestors to create a race with superior intelligence. Von Däniken examined the monuments, art, and artifacts of various cultures and claimed they represented spaceships and cosmic travelers. He observed the Nazca plains of Peru, where massive designs mark the ground, and pronounced they were extraterrestrial landing sites. Such colossal works as the pyramids of Egypt and the stone statues of Easter Island were built, he said, with the aid of technologically advanced visitors.

As proof of his theory, Erich von Däniken cited the writings of Ezekiel.

When Christians reject such interpretations of biblical accounts, UFO advocates turn to other sightings in historical records.

OTHER TIMES, OTHER SIGHTINGS

Some ancient documents contain references to strange sights in the sky—sights that today's ufologists are quick to label spacecraft. For example, the Chronicles of Alexander the Great report that his army was harassed by a pair of flying objects in 329 B.C. And in 1561 many citizens of the German city of Nuremberg witnessed disks that appeared in the sky to engage in an aerial ballet. Five years later, residents of Basel, Switzerland, saw a similar display. Edmond Halley, of comet fame, saw unexplained aerial objects in 1716. In 1881 two sons of the Prince of Wales saw illuminated ships in the sky off the coast of Australia.

The first wave of UFO sightings in the United States took place a hundred years ago. In the late 1890s thousands of people reported a mysterious cigar-shaped airship hovering over California. They described an object consisting of panels of glass or some transparent substance that emitted a brilliant white light. For several months newspapers followed the alleged movement of the strange craft as it meandered from the West Coast eastward. *Scientific American* called it a hoax. Others reported seeing downed airships piloted by eccentric inventors. The controversy ended less than a decade later when the Wright brothers flew the first airplane.

After the Ken Arnold sighting that coined the term *flying saucer,* investigators unearthed a similar description in a Texas newspaper article published by the *Denison Daily News* in 1878. According to that report, the craft "was about the size of a large saucer and was evidently at a great height."[4]

During World War II, American, German, and Japanese pilots reported phantom aircraft that were elliptical in shape. U.S. Air Force pilots flying over Germany in 1944 sighted eerie, luminous balls, which appeared out of nowhere to chase their planes. The fiery disks, some red, some orange, or white, toyed with the aircraft, occasionally blinking on-and-off like Christmas tree lights. As many as ten at a time tracked planes. The airmen called them "foo fighters," a name derived from a nonsense line in a *Smokey Stover* comic strip. "Where there's foo, there's fire," the comic character had said. (The French word *feu* means fire.)

From 1946 to 1948 a wave of UFO sightings occurred in Scandinavia. During one seven-month period, more than a thousand sightings were reported in Sweden alone. The crash of a UFO was reported in the cold, rocky terrain of Spitsbergen, a group of arctic islands more than five hundred miles north of Norway. Another space vehicle was said to have smashed into the earth in Poland and a live alien was pulled from the vehicle. It was taken to a hospital but died as doctors tried to remove its metal flight suit. The body was then purportedly shipped to the USSR.

In the United States, the Ken Arnold report was followed by comparable versions from people in scattered parts of the country. Some of the sightings occurred on the very day of Arnold's encounter; some preceded it. The UFO phenomenon now had a life of its own. In the early fifties, observers in North America claimed thousands of UFO sightings. Comedians and cartoonists, police and politicians, all commented on the sensation. Were these sightings real? Were the pilots hostile or friendly? Did they originate on Earth, or from the black vastness of space?

UFO sightings have not been the sole province of ordinary citizens. Credible accounts have come from military officers, commercial pilots, airport radar controllers, and even astronauts. The head of the British Astronomical Association described his experience in 1954 of seeing something that looked like "polished metal dinner plates."[5]

Unlike today's cultural climate, which gobbles up the incredible as fodder for talk shows and tabloids, the public attitude of the '40s and '50s was skeptical. Almost anyone who witnessed a UFO was held up to ridicule and professional ostracism, especially those in the scientific community. Thus interest in the issue was left to religious cults and amateur saucer buffs. It was not until the 1970s that the tide began to turn. In 1971 a poll by *Industrial Research* magazine revealed that 54 percent of scientists believed UFOs probably existed.

The air force collected data on the phenomenon and put the findings into what was called Project Blue Book, compiling 12,959 case studies from the years 1947 to 1969. Staff assigned each UFO report a case file number and organized it in a folder stamped TOP SECRET. They took detailed statements from witnesses, acquired photos, and wrote summaries, sometimes hundreds of pages in length.

Project Blue Book concluded that no sighting report gave any indication of being a threat to national security. Additionally, the air force argued that none of the sightings represented a technological characteristic beyond the range of current scientific knowledge. Most importantly, Project Blue Book declared there was absolutely no evidence indicating UFOs were the manifestation of extraterrestrial vehicles.

Official dismissals aside, reports of UFOs during the last forty years have increased, and the public's belief in alien existence has remained unabated. According to the latest survey, 40 percent of Americans think aliens have visited our planet.[6]

Been There, Done That

The vanguard of this belief that we are not alone in the universe has been led by those who not only say they have seen something out there, they claim to have actually been abducted by the occupants of spaceships.

A woman in Virginia named Clare says she has periodically been whisked away without warning by UFOs. Clare claims to have suffered through more than a hundred abductions by the occupants of a saucer-shaped vessel that touched down near her horse farm. She professes to have been poked and prodded, as well as to have undergone the taking of skin samples and the forced feeding of indiscernible substances.[7]

Clare's account sounds like the plot line for a bad B-grade movie. She was taken from bed while in a deep sleep and transported to an egg-shaped room. There she was pierced with needles and impregnated by creatures who periodically took the fetuses for experiments in spaceship nurseries. Understandably, Clare questions her sanity and says she lives in denial that it will happen again. But it always does.

Psychotic stories from a mentally disturbed woman? Not necessarily, according to the *Journal of Abnormal Psychology*. A professor of psychology at Carleton University in Ottawa, Canada, writing in the *Journal,* compared the intelligence, imagination, and hypnotic suggestibility of abductees and UFO sighters with the general population. The difference?

Basically only one—those experiencing UFO phenomena believed that extraterrestrial life existed *before* their harrowing experiences occurred.[8]

That conclusion is little comfort to Clare. Put yourself in her shoes. If UFO creatures are snatching you away for gruesome examinations, it is different from being diagnosed with a mental problem. If you're crazy, you can get professional help or emergency medical services. But don't try calling 911 to say you're being abducted by little green men from Mars. In Clare's case, perhaps the only thing worse than thinking you're crazy is believing you've been sexually assaulted by an extraterrestrial.

Clare is not alone in her dilemma. Mention being abducted by aliens, and a small group of folks will raise their hands to say they, too, have been there and done that. They currently number just over a thousand, but their numbers are growing by hundreds a year. They usually end up in the offices of a therapist who specializes in the hypnotic recovery of suppressed memories.

One such therapist, a Fairfax, Virginia, psychologist, describes the trauma of his patients. "It's not really a posttraumatic stress because it is an ongoing stress," the specialist explains. "This person is telling you it happened last night, and it's going to happen tomorrow."[9]

Other psychologists who study UFO abductees have argued that every one of them suffers from some psychological problem. The most frequently cited malady is "status deficiency," meaning that the person's position in life does not measure up to his expectations, so he manufactures tall tales to give himself importance.

I have personally encountered a dozen or so individuals who say they have seen UFOs in my more than twenty-five years of counseling spiritually oppressed persons. Like Clare, these people fear telling anyone about their exotic episodes. And despite their bizarre anecdotes, they are seemingly normal in other areas of their lives. But, like Clare, they dread the next abduction.

My investigations have concluded there are four possible explanations for such encounters with UFOs. First, some kind of alien being truly abducted these people and subjected them to terrifying experiments. Second, they suffered hallucinatory visions induced by drugs or by chemical and hormonal imbalances. Third, they were victims of satanic cults who know how to manipulate their victims' dissociative personalities to induce a perceived abduction. Finally, the incident was a demonic encounter in which the natural and the supernatural commingled.

The quest of this book is to determine what UFOs really are, where they come from, and which of these explanations is accurate. Let's begin by exploring a current discovery, which seems to validate life on other planets: the Martian meteorite.

CHAPTER THREE

Is There Really Life on Mars?

Do you remember what you were doing when you heard that President John F. Kennedy was assassinated?" That question was the defining moment for my generation. I do remember. I was standing at the top of the stairs on the second floor of the Sigma Alpha Epsilon fraternity house at the University of Nebraska. A guy yelled out the news from the first-floor lounge. Like the rest of my frat brothers, my jaw dropped. "It can't be true," we murmured to one another. Then we rushed to the lounge, where everyone had gathered to watch images on the black-and-white RCA Victor TV.

Through this tragic event, television changed from an entertainment medium to a window on the world. For the first time in history, millions of observers took part in a national tragedy. Television became a news maker as well as a reporter.

Like President Kennedy's assassination, the defining question of the current generation could be: "Where were you when you first heard they found life on Mars?" Once again, I know where I was—in my office on a warm summer morning, reading the August 8, 1996, cover story "Was There Life On Mars?" in *USA Today*. The headline put the auspiciousness of the moment into perspective: "Discovery would equal finding the New World." The article heralded the finding of a tubular structure, which resembled a fossil, on a rock believed to have landed on Earth from Mars.

Over the next several weeks nearly every major magazine hailed the finding. "Come in, Mars," a *Newsweek* headline blared.[1] "Life on Mars," *Time* claimed in a cover story.[2] "New Traces of Past Life on Mars," The *New York Times* reported.[3] President Clinton added, "I am determined that the American space program will put its full intellectual power and technological prowess behind the search for further evidence. If the discovery is confirmed, it will surely be one of the most stunning insights into our universe that science has ever uncovered."[4]

Could such prestigious sources be wrong? Surely they had checked out all the facts. If it were now proven that life exists on Mars, what of my faith in God, who I believed gave the sons of Adam a privileged place in the universe? Could I no longer consider humans the only stewards of His creation and the uniquely privileged heirs of His salvation? I faced a dilemma.

There are other questions to answer. Why does life exist? Was creation or evolution the cause? Was there a finite beginning by the hand of an intelligent Creator or did cosmic elements congeal over millions of eons to form a molecule somewhere, or several somewheres?

Let's begin answering these questions by exploring the facts that undergird the assumption that there is life on Mars.

THE ORIGINS OF "THE ROCK"

In 1994 scientists at NASA's Johnson Space Center in Houston obtained part of a 4.1-pound, potato-shaped meteorite found in Antarctica a decade earlier. They compared its chemical analysis with information gathered by the *Viking* missions to Mars in the 1970s to conclude that the stone was Martian. They dated it at 4.5 billion years old, the oldest of twelve known Martian meteorites found on Earth.

The meteorite, called Allan Hills 84001 (ALH84001), was believed to have been knocked into space by an asteroid collision on Mars sixteen million years ago. It crashed into the Allan Hills region of Antarctica thirteen thousand years ago. Upon examination of the meteorite, its tiny tubular and egg-shaped structures, resembling fossils of bacteria-like organisms, looked suspiciously similar to organisms found among early life-forms on Earth. Scientists reported seeing microscopic worms clutching the underside of the rust-colored rock. These, they concluded, were carbonate mineral globules containing tiny grains of chemicals, and they were almost identical to fossil remnants left by certain bacteria found on Earth.

Since all life as we know it is carbon-based, these globules were dubbed "life." NASA certainly did not discover little green men—just some carbon molecules similar to fossilized bacteria. So were these assumptions equivalent to the sailing of the *Niña*, the *Pinta*, and the *Santa Maria*? Were they as momentous as the pronouncement of Copernicus four centuries ago, when he discovered that the Earth is not the center of the universe?

Some scientists are not so sure. If the discovered material is organic, does it actually contain fossil remains? Are they fossils at all? The oldest fossils on Earth are 4.3-billion-year-old microscopic worms found in Australia. These Martian worms are said to be a little younger, 3.6 billion years old. The Martian "fossils" are one-thousandth the diameter of a human hair, one hundred times smaller than the oldest fossils found on Earth. Does this truly qualify as life? Do the fossils have the cell walls needed to hold the stuff of life? There is apparently no way to slice the fossil sample and find out, because the so-called fossils are too minuscule to be analyzed chemically or probed internally.

With so much inconclusive information, is the presumed finding of life on our red neighbor a colossal Martian mistake? Scientists have previously discovered the stuff found in the Allan Hill meteorite in other interplanetary debris, and they have never before interpreted it as biological. Could the push to call this latest discovery "life" be the result of a social agenda rather than a scientific pursuit? None of the alleged fossils had the semblance of a cell or any evidence of cell division. UCLA paleobiologist William Schopf, best known for discovering the world's oldest fossils, said the structures NASA was touting as fossilized life-forms were probably made of "mineralic material" like dried mud. "The biological explanation is unlikely," he concluded.[5]

Could this discovery have a religious and philosophical motivation as well?

The Rock Theory
Is a Little Rocky

Just as creationists believe that God was there in the beginning to get everything going, evolutionists are determined to prove their ideas about life's origins are accurate. I believe the majority of scientists have an anti-Christian bias. They are predisposed to find life somehow, somewhere other than Earth in order to once and for all silence the Genesis account.

Witness the hasty conclusions of those from all walks of life who have a philosophically vested interest in making the dream of life on Mars come true:

- Deceased atheist astronomer Carl Sagan: "If the results are verified, it is a turning point in human history."[6]

- Distinguished Rice University historian of astronomy, Albert van Helden: "If it turns out to be true, it would be a compelling demonstration that life on Earth is not unique."[7]

- Former particle physicist and New Age metaphysician Fritjof Capra: "If confirmed, the finding shows that the cosmos is alive. This view should engender a different attitude toward the natural world."[8]

With so many important people so excited, it is wise to recount how scientists surmise the life-bearing Martian rocks came to Earth. Keep in mind that no one was there to actually observe the events; however, that lack of observability has never bothered those of the Darwinian persuasion. Their version surmises that nearly four billion years ago water covered the Martian surface. Microbes flourished in these seas and eventually fossilized in the cracks of rocks. Then millions of years ago (sixteen million years is the speculative time frame), a giant asteroid slammed into Mars and exploded with the power of a million hydrogen bombs. Huge quantities of rock were flung into the Martian atmosphere. Because of the blast's force, some rocks were expelled from Mars with enormous speed and went into orbit around the sun.

Then thirteen thousand years ago, as Stone Age Neanderthals pursued a woolly mammoth, they looked up and witnessed a fiery meteor blaze across the sky. It nearly burned to total disintegration, except for a small spud-sized portion, which plunged into the Antarctic ice cap. In 1994 scientists came upon the rock. At the time they did not realize they held the key to discrediting the Christian teaching of geocentricism, that man and this planet are the living center of the universe. But that was certainly the headline news in 1996, when word of the discovery was widely publicized.

Think about this for a minute. The scenario accepted by the life-on-Mars advocates is not based on empirical evidence. It is based on deductive conclusions drawn from postulations that require as much faith as believing Hebrews 11:3, which says, "By faith we understand that the worlds were framed by the word of God, so that the things which are seen were not made of things which are visible."

As I have contemplated this Martian meteorite, and the effect its findings have on my faith in God and the Bible, I have come to several conclusions. First, no scientist can state without equivocation that ALH84001 came from Mars. No rock from Mars has ever been brought from that planet and held in human hands. The theory of the Martian rock's interplanetary journey to Earth is a hypothetical explanation, not an observed phenomenon.

Second, even if the rock is from Mars, it is almost impossible to conclude that it managed to avoid earthly contamination. Stanford's Richard Zare, the scientist who conducted the polycyclic aromatic hydrocarbon research into this aspect of the issue, says contamination is "not likely." But I ask you:

Should mankind so readily discard the biblical teaching of man's centrality to the universe on the basis of a "not likely" conclusion?

Let's ask another question: How did those tiny worms get inside the rock? Scientists say they crawled in there when the rock was part of the red planet's crust. The late Carl Sagan was ecstatic at that assumption: "This was a time when Mars was warmer and wetter than it is today, with rivers, lakes, and possibly even oceans."[9] (Isn't it amazing how Sagan could reject the biblical story of Eden but so readily adopt as fact a fanciful rendering of what might have happened on Mars several billion years ago?)

EVOLUTIONARY UPDATE

Perhaps the most startling question being asked by scientists today is this: Was the cosmos seeded with life?

Are they serious? Yes, they are. Having rejected the idea of divine intervention as the source of life on Earth, some scientists are using the Martian microbes as an excuse to say that life on Earth may have actually originated on Mars. One eminent chemist enjoined in the life-on-Mars debate has gone so far as to suggest, "Who is to say that we are not all Martians?"[10]

This zany opinion is similar to an even more radical theory known as panspermia, the supposition that billions of years ago the solar system was showered with the seeds of biological life, which took root wherever conditions were right. Proponents of this outrageous idea do not bother to ask the obvious question: Where did the seeds come from, and who, or what, flung them throughout the universe?

Even scientists who reject the panspermia suggestion have adjusted their evolutionary outlook to include the possibility of life on Earth having early extraterrestrial origins. In other words, organic chemicals and amino acids hitched a ten-million-year-long ride on a passing meteor and found a home on Earth. This speculative Mars-seeded-Earth idea holds sway over some scientists who would be embarrassed to be seen reading a Bible.

As I consider these explanations of life's origins, I must decide if God's Word means what it says or if it requires a metaphysical interpretation. For example, when Jesus said in John 14:2, "In My Father's house are many mansions," was He suggesting that humankind lives in one small corner of a more vast and varied tenant complex? Even if the Martian microbes are accepted as some sort of life-form, these fossil traces are still far removed from humanity. After all, if God had wanted life to arise on Mars, surely He could have done better than bacterial worms.

Some might say that my insistence of Earthman's centrality in the universe is the result of egoism, based on my human sense of self-importance. But I believe that Adam and Eve were masters of the universe because God put them in charge of all that He made. They were not insignificant beings on only one speck of solar dust.

Frank Drake, professor of astronomy and astrophysics at the University of California, Santa Cruz, has written a book entitled *Is Anyone Out There?* assuring readers that life exists on other planets. Drake concludes that since there are another two hundred billion galaxies like ours, "The evidence supports the idea that there are almost countless systems of living things in the universe. There are perhaps tens of thousands of civilizations in our galaxy and even more abodes of more primitive life. Everything we know about the formation and the evolution of the solar system, planets and of life on Earth says that the whole sequence of events was the result of completely normal and, in fact, inevitable processes. So what happened in our solar system and on Earth should have happened in many, many places."[11]

This type of reasoning compels scientists to look for life out there, anywhere.

LIFE BEYOND MARS

A week after NASA announced that Mars may once have harbored life, scientists said that one of Jupiter's moons, icy Europa, showed signs that it might be warm enough and wet enough to support life. Images from the *Galileo* space probe showed that Europa's crust had broken and shifted on a lubricating layer of some kind, perhaps a tier of warm water. A scientist tracking the *Galileo* project presumptuously declared that cracks on Europa's surface "are places that would be environmentally favorable for life."[12]

Astronomers also recently found two planets orbiting stars outside our solar system. Scientists guessed that one of them might be able to support life, and dubbed it Goldilocks, because it had a temperature that was "just right." (Both planets are only forty light years from Earth.) Goldilocks is six times as massive as Jupiter and, according to a professor of physics and astronomy at San Francisco State University, might have water, which could "exist in a liquid form . . . which would lead to life."[13]

All such conjecture implicitly poses the question: What are we doing here? Scientists who try to identify life beyond Earth are not much different from the myth makers of old. In the superstitious past, pagans believed that the sky was the source of omens and prophecies. The Mayas of the Yucatan eyed the planets with an animistic intent and imagined agricultural deities warning of floods and droughts. The ancient Chinese focused on Mars as the home of gods who could foretell their future. Since the seventeenth century, when the telescope was developed, stargazers have probed the heavens for signs of life in stellar dust. The question still remains: Is life on Earth a fluke, or the product of intelligent design?

What Matters About Mars

Atheists say that Christians and theologians ignore the possibilities of life on other planets because that finding would destroy our beliefs. They also say that we center our biological assumptions on a single point of data—life as we know it. But you have to throw out all assumptions about life in this discussion, they say, because life "out there" may be very different from life here.

But if someone is out there and these space invaders pay us a visit to share a spiritual cosmology different from the Judeo-Christian one, what then? That has already happened. Abductees of aliens relate that their captors have done just that. Aliens are preaching a "different gospel"—a message very different from the gospel of Jesus Christ. A careful analysis of the pronouncements from these space creatures shows that their inclination is to the occult, not Christianity. That guilt by association tells us a great deal about their origins—and maybe something about their motives.

It is important to establish my point of view when discussing UFOs and extraterrestrial phenomena. My philosophical foundation is my belief in the Bible as the Word of God. This framework determines how I view the world in which I live and the worlds of outer space that man has not yet explored.

When I first accepted Christianity, my decision was both intellectual and emotional. Intellectually I had to determine whether Christ's death on the cross and His resurrection were historical facts to be acknowledged; however, the compelling motive for my commitment to Christ was from the heart. I was moved by the Holy Spirit to my very core, where the love of God touched my soul. At that point there was no mental debate, only a heartfelt response.

I found God the old-fashioned way. I had gone off to college and was planning on a career in medicine. As a university student my thinking was information-based. I loved research. But my life changed one night. It was a chilly winter's eve. I had come to town to visit my parents. Some friends asked me to join them for a gospel service in a small Kansas church, just over the state line from my hometown. I was hesitant at first because I had not been inside a church in years. I felt drawn that night, though I don't recall much of what was said. What I do remember is feeling as though I was ready to start crying as I listened to the speaker talk about his conversion to Christ.

At the conclusion of his message, he issued a public invitation for those who wished to accept the Lord to come to the altar. Everyone watched in amazement as I walked down the aisle. I knelt at the front of the church and something inside me broke. I wept for the years I had failed to let God control my life. I felt relieved to give the burden of guilt to God and repented of my sins. That night I vowed that, by His grace, I would put the Lord first in my life from that day forward.

The spiritual journey since then has been filled with many ups and downs. But whatever the circumstances, my trust in God has matured and become less emotional and more thoughtful. The longer I serve the Lord, the more I learn and can expand the intellectual basis for my beliefs. That shifting balance, from feelings to reason, has a direct bearing on why I wrote this book.

To me, the importance of UFOs, their origin and purpose, is not a matter of opinion based on the latest "scientific" evidence. I believe in the authority of Scripture, and I am obligated to evaluate all phenomena on the basis of biblical revelation. Because the issue of UFOs has a bearing on explanations regarding the origins of man and his place in the universe, I must render a theological judgment on the subject. I believe the presence of UFOs is due to another force science cannot investigate, a conclusion this book is written to establish.

Scripture clearly teaches the cosmological consequences of Adam and Eve's fall. What happened in the province of Eden affected everything God created in Genesis 1:1 ("the heavens and the earth"). Romans 8:21–22 puts it this way: "the creation itself also will be delivered from the bondage of corruption into the glorious liberty of the children of God. For we know that the *whole creation* groans and labors with birth pangs" (emphasis added).

All the universe is tainted by the rebellion of our First Parents. The second law of thermodynamics bears this out scientifically. It states that our universe is afflicted by a state of entropy, that it is dying and slowly disintegrating toward a state of disorder. This chaos is the result of man's spiritual rebellion. In like manner, because of sin, all that exists is degenerating spiritually and is in need of reconciliation to God. This would include any intelligent creature on any planet and in any galaxy.

Let me raise some additional complications to the popular assumptions regarding UFOs and extraterrestrial aliens. If beings in outer space exist, and they are capable of contacting us, how could they circumvent the effect of sin? If the retrogressive aftermath of sin has robbed us of Eden's perfection and has limited our technological abilities to travel to other planets, wouldn't these aliens be just as restricted? If the issue of universal entropy is sidestepped, and we assume these aliens were not affected by Adam's sin, then why would God permit beings who have not sinned to contact us and be affected by our moral transgressions?

If we adopt the premise that the entire cosmos has been spiritually contaminated by original sin, then any aliens would be as much in need of a Savior as we who are citizens of Earth. To take that a step further, did Christ appear as God made in the form of man only on Earth, or did Christ also take on the form of alien flesh? Is Jesus the Redeemer of earthbound humans alone, or was He crucified again and again in distant worlds? These ridiculous, rhetorical questions grow exponentially.

After studying this issue for more than twenty years, I have concluded that admitting to the existence of life anywhere beyond our biosphere, whether it is a bacterium on Mars or an alien in a flying saucer, undermines the paradigm upon which my faith is based. If life, especially sentient life capable of consciousness, exists anywhere outside of God's earthly realm, then mankind's humanness is not all that special. Some Christians may not agree with that deduction, but I believe it is because they have not adequately examined the facts.

THE SPIRITUAL BATTLE

To understand the magnitude of this Martian matter, the significance of the Incarnation must be understood. The Bible views Christ as the son of Adam (Luke 3:38), His human identity as the seed of Earth's first man. Christ experienced the complete range of human experiences: compassion (Matt. 9:36), love (John 11:36), surprise (Matt. 8:10), pain (Luke 22:44), thirst (John 19:28), and death (John 19:30).

But Jesus was more than a mere man. His miracles displayed authority over creation. In Matthew 8:26, He calmed the seas with His spoken word. Matthew 14:19–21 tells how He multiplied the loaves and fishes. Colossians 1:16 describes Jesus Christ as the Creator of the universe. The mystery of the Incarnation is that Jesus, who was fully God, came to Earth as a man—a baby crying in His mother's arms and a falsely condemned criminal on a cross. Remaining at one with—and equal to—God, He took the form of a slave, to share our sorrows and atone for our sins.

It is in the Atonement that we see the real reason for the incarnation of Christ. Hebrews 10:4–7 speaks of His bodily offering for sin ("Sacrifice and offering You did not desire,/ but a body You have prepared for Me"). The guilt of our sin required a God-man to die for our salvation. In the Incarnation we see God's rich mercy identifying with the day-by-day sufferings of humanity. Paul wrote of the Incarnation, "that though He was rich, yet for your sakes He became poor, that you through His poverty might become rich" (2 Cor. 8:9). Thus the Incarnation and the Atonement are inseparable. Any theory or scientific postulation which lessens the significance of Christ becoming the God-man devalues the emphasis God places on our worth as His creation.

The scientific willingness to accept extraterrestrial life, in any form, is a reflection of the spiritual diversity of our times. With Eastern mystical ideas and New Age occult teachings so rampant, it is only logical that scientists would color their conclusions by these models. The cosmologies of the East, such as Hinduism, have all kinds of alternate universes inhabited by ascended beings. Buddhists and Taoists leave room for any number of deities and demigods roaming the galaxies at will.

The Judeo-Christian tradition is set apart from all these

views of the cosmos. The revelation of God on Mount Sinai was for the wanderers of the Exodus, not aliens on Mars. The death of Christ on Golgotha was a time-space event for the progeny of Adam and Eve. Having considered all the evidence, the intellectual basis for my faith stands sure. I reject the theory that life on Earth arose from a zillion-to-one accidental arrangement of molecules. I also repudiate the notion that the very vastness of the universe necessitates accepting the statistical possibility of alien life.

The truth is this: We are not just involved in a scientific debate; we are involved in a spiritual battle.

The battle lines of an immense spiritual struggle are before us. On one side the infidel determination of science is abetted by popular culture, including science fiction literature and films.

Standing against this atheistic onslaught are those of us with a biblical worldview, who conclude that we are living in the Last Days. We believe this is the hour prophesied by the apostle Peter, who warned that scoffers would come denying that the worlds were made by God (2 Peter 3:3–7).

However compelling our arguments, we cannot expect the proponents of extraterrestrial life to run up the white flag and surrender. This is a battle to the end—the end of time.

And from the front lines of this battle, thunderous salvos can be heard from the movie machine of Hollywood.

CHAPTER FOUR

UFOs and Hollywood Hype

When I was about seven years old, my family took a summer vacation to California. We drove from Nebraska to San Francisco, and then on to the northern part of the state. It was a weeklong trip filled with bathroom stops, counting cars, and reading the Burma Shave signs that dotted the highways.

Every afternoon during our road trip, we tuned through the static on the AM dial to find a local radio station carrying the congressional investigations underway. At that early age I understood little of what was going on, except that an enemy called communism was trying to destroy our way of life and Senator Joe McCarthy was determined to prevent it.

The world in those days was inhabited by people who trusted other people; and, for the most part, they trusted their government. There was no pejorative label called "McCarthyism" to cynically describe official efforts at witch hunts. We naively believed that McCarthy and his congressional cohorts would do the right thing and protect our country from subversive forces.

Today, things are different. Few people trust those in authority, government scandals are old news, and the 1950s fear of an alien political ideology halfway around the globe has given way to a paranoia about alien space invaders a galaxy away. Many believe that our elected officials have lied to us about black helicopters on secret missions and dead alien bodies kept from public view. In other words, we have met the enemy and he is us—our own government.

Hollywood has been quick to exploit this national misgiving on television and the big screen.

Big Screen Space Invaders

Over the last two decades I have noted the success of UFO movies and television shows with great curiosity. I was not a *Star Trek* devotee of the William Shatner era, nor have I been hooked by the "next generation" varieties. I did take serious note of the *Star Wars* trilogy, and I have seen most of the popular science fiction movies.

Our cultural captivation with the possibility of life on other planets is so intense that the biggest movie hits are related to UFOs. *E.T.—the Extraterrestrial* was the most popular film of all time until it was displaced by *Star Wars,* financially enhanced by its 1997 return to the big screen. *Independence Day, The Empire Strikes Back, Return of the Jedi,* and *Close Encounters of the Third Kind* all made the top ten list.

Some may be bored by movies about UFOs, sick of hearing about sightings, and consider those obsessed with extraterrestrials to be mentally imbalanced. But no one can live on this planet and escape the effect of the Hollywood hype.

HYNEK AND THE HYPE

Today's Martian movie mayhem got its first major economic vote of confidence in 1977 with Steven Spielberg's *Close Encounters of the Third Kind.* Richard Dreyfuss played an ordinary family man, named Roy Neary, who was psychically drawn toward an alien encounter. While those around him, including his wife and children, were ignorant of the suprarational communications he was receiving, Neary graduated from fascination to fixation. Even a pile of mashed potatoes on his dinner plate became a signal from beyond, calling him to meet with those who had chosen him as their contactee. (The potatoes, it turns out, remotely resembled the alien landing site at Devil's Tower, Wyoming.)

The film drew its strength from a focus on man's universal fascination with epiphany and magic, presented in an atmosphere of innocence. This theme was most obvious in the final scenes when the alien ship arrived in a flurry of harmonious colors and sound. Dumbfounded humans were treated to a light show without rival and to a concert that introduced them to the universal cosmic language of tones. When the aliens finally appeared, they were not monsters but nonthreatening, embryonic children. Earth people responded with wonder and joy at the sight of such amiable muses.

The tension between rationality and irrationality in *Close Encounters* was emphasized by a character in the film, a French scientist who fought against those debunking UFOs. This role was a none-too-thinly veiled reference to Jacques Vallee, the prominent French astrophysicist and ufologist. UFO buffs revere Vallee, though he generally dismisses the idea of aliens coming from other solar systems. His theory is that UFOs are interdimensional, that is, they are manifestations of a "parallel reality."

Throughout the film Neary was caught between his intellectual logic and the aliens' occult spirituality. At the end of the movie, metaphysics won, and Neary solemnly strolled toward the spaceship to meet the unknown aliens. As he stepped aboard, a movie voice-over from an unidentified source intoned the reassuring words of Psalm 91:11: "He shall give His angels charge over you."

An important guiding hand of *Close Encounters* was the scientist who served as a technical advisor, the late Dr. J. Allen Hynek, professor of astronomy at Northwestern University. In 1948 the air force asked Hynek to investigate flying saucers. At the time he thought the idea was a fad, but as the years progressed he became convinced there was something to the phenomenon.

When the government refused to further investigate the seven hundred cases that seemed to indicate genuine UFO encounters in Project Blue Book, Hynek became convinced the authorities wanted to stonewall the UFO mystery because it made the air force look ineffective. After all, if the Pentagon took billions of dollars in taxes every year to defend the United States against all foreign enemies and appeared helpless against an unidentified invader, congressional appropriations could suffer.

After thirty-five years of extraterrestrial research, Hynek concluded that UFO appearances represented contact with some form of intelligence, and that the encounters were purposely staged. Hynek published a bimonthly *International UFO Reporter* to provide coverage of these events. He also founded and directed the Center for UFO Studies. His UFO classification system, the basis for the title of Spielberg's movie, sorted sightings according to four basic kinds of "close encounters":

- First Kind—An observer sees a UFO within five hundred feet.

- Second Kind—The UFO leaves some sort of physical trace behind, such as a marking on the ground, interference with electrical activity like television and radio reception, or physical signs of burning and charring.

- Third Kind—A person actually sees the occupants of the UFO, in or near the spacecraft.

- Fourth Kind—The aliens abduct and/or examine the person.

Other methods of categorizing UFOs are even more complex, such as Jacques Vallee's system, which examines whether the UFO is associated with spirits (ascended masters or higher beings) or a paranormal entity (a source of intelligence). Vallee is especially concerned with instances in which the observer actually traveled out of his body into the craft through astral projection.

These close encounters of the third and fourth kinds, which involve metaphysical contact with aliens, seem to interest Hollywood the most. Anyone can say they've seen a saucer, but actually boarding one, or speaking with its inhabitants, is much more sensational.

E. T. PHONE HOME

Many Americans empathized with the poignant line of Spielberg's lovable alien who sorrowfully said, "E. T. phone home." This extraterrestrial so longed for contact with his stellar family that he fashioned an interplanetary communications device from an umbrella, a Speak-and-Spell game, and the blade of a circular saw. No one begrudged his reaching out to touch someone, somewhere. It can get a little lonely when you're three million light years from family and friends.

Released in 1982, the movie *E.T.* produced profits approaching a billion dollars! When it hit video stores six years after the initial release, it sold eight million copies the first day. Scores of spin-off licenses brought in billions of dollars more from video games, bicycles, pajamas, calendars, masks—you name it. Who would have dreamed that this gray-green polyurethane humanoid with a ten-word vocabulary would end up with his own ride at Universal Studios' entertainment complex?

Contrary to popular perception, *E.T.* was more than an updated form of *Buck Rogers* adventurism. I believe that *E.T.* was carefully crafted to sell the public on the acceptance of alien life. Early in Spielberg's career, he said, "I unequivocally think there is life in other solar systems in our galaxy. I've never seen a UFO, but . . . I really am waiting my turn. I would love to see something that can't be explained by science or logic."[1]

The plot of *E.T.* was simple enough. A deco-styled spaceship full of otherworldly creatures landed in a misty forest that abutted suburbia. The aliens were there to collect samples of Earth's botanical life. One of the invaders was a four-fingered, web-footed, interplanetary immigrant with froglike eyes. Eliot, the film's cute kid played by Henry Thomas, gave this alien the name "E. T."

Unfortunately, E. T. lingered too long among the flora, and the other aliens left him behind when their craft departed abruptly. Eliot discovered the three-foot, six-inch creature and, with the help of his older brother, Michael, and younger sister, Gertie, concealed E. T. in the closet to protect him from the prying eyes of adults.

Several supernatural scenes propelled the story. Eliot's psychic attachment to his newfound friend was so strong that Eliot felt everything E. T. did, including E. T.'s drunken encounter with Coors. Apparently both were in touch with some universal mind beyond human consciousness. When Eliot cut his finger, one of E.T.'s digits glowed red. The mini-monster then healed Eliot's hand instantly. In several other scenes E. T. performed acts of levitation, suggesting that gravitational hindrances do not apply to beings with advanced understanding.

Eventually E. T. longed for home, but by then he had been discovered by nasty government investigators who sent a cadre of scientists to examine the alien visitor. Toward the end of the movie, E. T. died and was subsequently resurrected from the dead by Eliot's love for him. Eliot immediately whisked E. T. away to the returned spaceship in a madcap chase scene, which pitted childhood spunk against know-nothing bureaucrats.

The most spiritually disturbing moment of the film took place as the two friends parted: E. T. pointed to the center of Eliot's forehead and comforted his grieving friend with the consolation, "I'll be right here." I suspect that E. T. was pointing to the third eye, the presumed psychic center of telepathic perception. E. T. was telling Eliot that they could maintain their spiritually sympathetic communication even though galaxies apart.

The theme of the movie was obvious: psychokinetic powers are superior to the human faculties of speech and reason. I wonder how many children may have actually looked for extradimensional spirit beings because of *E.T.*'s message that the accumulated intelligence of the millennia and the supernatural powers of the occult reside in extraterrestrials?

Some movie aliens, like E. T., are friendly companions, but others are ready to wage war.

THE ULTIMATE ALIEN INVASION

The movie *Independence Day (ID4)* was not the first alien invasion on celluloid, but it made the most money of any film with that theme. Unlike *Close Encounters* and *E.T.,* the extraterrestrials of *ID4* were not friendly. They were on a mission—the end of the world, including an obliteration of the White House.

The movie's plot began on July 2 in the near future when humongous spaceships entered the Earth's atmosphere. They hovered over fifteen major cities and sent out rays that pulverized Washington, New York, Los Angeles, Paris, and Moscow. The next day the U.S. president plotted a counterattack with the aid of a computer genius. On July 4, Independence Day, the two civilizations entered a climactic dogfight. Tens of millions were dead, but hope lived on in the hands of a psychic president, an Air Force macho man, and a drunken crop duster.

ID4 was not a subtle film. Mass destruction prevailed before a third of the movie was underway. The actors were almost incidental to the state-of-the-art aerial combat scenes, complete with more miniature models of cities, alien aircraft, helicopters, and fighter jets than any movie before.

The moral paucity of the film was confirmed by the unnecessarily frequent use of profanity and blasphemy. Most alien-oriented movies have been scripted for childhood consumption, but the heroine in this movie was a stripper whose behavior was excused because she cared about her kid. The hero was a loud and proud fighter pilot, though he slept with the stripper and had no serious interest in marrying her until the aliens arrived. An obligatory whiny gay guy, played by Harvey Fierstein, seemed as likable as he did irritating.

Considering the spiritual significance of its apocalyptic events, *ID4* hardly mentioned religion. And the only references to Christianity were not honorable. Even the U.S. president constantly used God's name in vain. The only serious allusion to faith was the comment of a Jewish man who said he had been mad at God and had not talked to Him since his wife died.

In contrast to the subject of religion, the characters in *Independence Day* referred to psychic phenomena deferentially; for instance, scientists said the aliens were "like us" because they communed with each other by "ESP and mental telepathy." The truth is that only those involved in the occult indulge in such paranormal forms of communication.

Two of the most important characters, portrayed by Randy Quaid and Jeff Goldblum, were drunks. No one in the movie had a shred of moral fiber, and yet they prevailed over the descending spaceships to save the Earth. As a destruction derby, *ID4* was impressive, but fifteen-mile-wide death ships and a president who can read the minds of aliens could not save the movie from its tacky characters and its predictable plot line. At the end of the film, what was left of America was saved, with no questions answered about where the spaceships came from or when they might be back. Do I detect a sequel?

With the nation's increasing appetite for the extraterrestrial, Hollywood studios have a camera-ready formula. They have reincarnated Sigourney Weaver in yet another feminist-versus-horrific-creatures *Aliens* movie. Michael Jordan briefly left the basketball court to throw hoops in *Space Jam*, and studios have even resurrected *My Favorite Martian*. Warner Brothers alone has churned out five recent films about aliens.

As this book is being written, a dozen or so major tinseltown sci-fi productions are in progress, in addition to those already on the screen and on video (John Travolta's *Phenomenon*, Charlie Sheen's *The Arrival*, and the latest in the *Star Trek* series, *First Contact*, to name a few).

In most cases, these silver-screen aliens are not friendly, except for *Contact*, based on the late Carl Sagan's bestseller. This movie has attracted wealthy financial backers, a prestigious director (Robert Zemeckis of *Forrest Gump* fame), and well-known actors, including Jodie Foster. The film portrays a benign race of aliens, apparently close cousins to the extraterrestrials of Steven Spielberg's *Close Encounters of the Third Kind*.

Science fiction has always been a mainstay of cinema. According to industry experts, besides soap opera fans and country music fanatics, no other followers are as loyal. Who else regularly turns up at hotel conventions, like the *Star Trek* events, all over the country?

And television is just as crowded with UFOs and paranormal subjects. NBC has been surprised by its hit *Third Rock from the Sun* and has followed up with the more serious *Dark Skies*. Fox has capitalized on the link between aliens and the supernatural with its fare, including *Sliders*, *Poltergeist: The Legacy*, *Sightings*, *Millennium*, and *The X-Files*. Other networks have added *The Sentinel* and *The Outer Limits*, to name a few examples of this recent trend.

The Fear and Loathing of UFOs on Film

As I have shown above, Hollywood cannot seem to make up its mind about the aims of aliens. Are they benevolent beings with advanced spiritual understanding (*E.T.* and *Close Encounters*), or are they loathsome creatures who despise the human race and want to destroy the Earth (*Independence Day*)?

At times the entertainment industry shows unknown aliens as frightening intruders with evil intentions. In the original "War of the Worlds," death rays from descending ships zapped everything in sight. In *It Came from Outer Space* the interlopers landed and took over human bodies. The beings Sigourney Weaver eluded in the *Aliens* episodes were as frightful as anything ever conceived in the horror genre. Even Disney World has jumped on the evil-alien bandwagon, revamping Tomorrowland to include an attraction called ExtraTERRORestrial Encounter.

At other times, movie directors seem to tell us that extraterrestrial life is not just benign, but messianic. We must welcome the appearance of aliens as if they heralded a Christlike Second Coming, a compassionate intervention to save man from himself. In *Close Encounters* whimsical creatures communicated with musical notes. E. T. charmed his young friends, and his kindly nature was contrasted with the ruthlessness of the humans tracking him.

What is the truth according to the entertainment media? Should aliens be loved or loathed? From Hollywood's perspective, who knows? All we can be certain of is that the film industry's idea of how we envision UFOs may change from year to year. Hollywood's flip-flops are probably a reflection of the changing ways in which Americans see themselves.

After long observation of the contradictory themes of Hollywood's exploitation of UFOs, I have concluded that our current fascination with the topic has taken a major philosophical deviation. In the past, when movie aliens were always evil, there was something cathartic about these potent parables. Aliens were dangerous, but we could conquer them through hope and the American way. If necessary, we could go after them—out there.

Then Neil Armstrong stepped on the moon and dispelled some of the mystery of our universe. We knew how far we could go, but we also decided we probably could not go much farther. If contact were to be made with outer space beings, they would have to come to us. We turned from being challengers in the battle for the control of the universe and became bystanders. With the exception of the aggressive *Star Trek* approach, most movies showed us waiting for the next extraterrestrial visitor to drop by. Meanwhile, we hoped they would treat us kindly.

The upshot of all UFO-oriented films is that some kind of life must exist somewhere and those of us on Earth are pretty insignificant in the cosmic scheme of things. That may be the unkindest cut of all because it says something about mankind's twentieth-century inferiority complex.

According to a *Newsweek* poll, 48 percent of Americans believe UFOs are real and 29 percent think we have made contact with aliens. Forty-eight percent also think there is a government plot to cover up the whole thing. This public overconfidence in things paranormal is so strong that three men were arrested in the spring of 1996 on New York's Long Island for plotting to assassinate local officials; the men believed the authorities had concealed a UFO landing. Strange stuff? That's tame compared to some less than reputable stargazers who claim to have seen Elvis eating fried chicken on the planet Uranus![2]

When *USA Today* asked its readers if they believed that life exists in other parts of the universe, the majority said yes.

Interestingly, most of them also thought that extraterrestrial life probably looked a lot like us.[3] In other words, we believe the Hollywood stories that someone is out there; however, we want whomever it is to resemble the image in our mirrors.

Perhaps the science fiction obsession is not a telescope seeking alien worlds but a microscope peering into our own consciousness. From *Invasion of the Body Snatchers* to *2001: A Space Odyssey* the subject matter may be a metaphor for our own dark souls. We do not want to be our brother's keepers, so we superstitiously speculate that our problem is a powerful interplanetary menace beyond our power to control. That way we can evade taking personal responsibility for methodically solving the problems in our midst. Instead, we seem to have made an unconscious decision to passively await the next invasion of aliens—not knowing whether they will be killers or messiahs.

A few UFO enthusiasts, however, are not waiting so passively. They are gathering in conferences to discuss their experiences with aliens, and even to contact the "space brothers" for advice.

CHAPTER FIVE

New Age Nuttiness and Psychic Phenomena

Hundreds of skeptics and believers converged on Colorado State University in Fort Collins, Colorado, for a five-day conference on reincarnation, psychic healing, and extraterrestrials. The gathering, not officially sanctioned by the university, was the brainchild of a CSU engineering professor. Discussion groups talked about alien abductions, out-of-body experiences and dowsing (using a forked hazel stick to locate underground water, minerals, or missing persons).

The conference was also an outgrowth of student curiosity. A college course on reincarnation stimulated so much interest that students from a group called FLAG (Former Life Action Group), which evolved into another group called SPRE (Society for Psi Research and Education), sponsored the event. What happened on the Colorado campus is a microcosm for America's fascination with all things paranormal.

Today's interest in the other-worldly goes beyond the idea that aliens built Atlantis or that sewer-dwelling dwarfs have kidnapped missing children. First Lady Hillary Clinton has imaginary conversations with the dead. Designer Donna Karan says that in previous lives she was a cowgirl and a painter in the court of the Medicis. The paranormal has its dabblers and devotees, but it also has sober researchers who eagerly investigate the possibility that the mind affects matter. Entertainment industry giant Sony has even set up a lab to run ESP experiments.

Corporations like Sony can expect a good return on their paranormal investments, because those enamored with psychic powers flock to see films like *Phenomenon*. In the movie, a blinding bolt from the sky strikes John Travolta's character, George Malley. The film never makes it clear that the encounter is extraterrestrial, but George's intellectual capacities and his telekinetic abilities take a quantum leap into another dimension.

George instantly speaks languages he never learned before by merely holding a book in his hands. He immediately absorbs a book on physics while turning the pages without touching them. When a doctor examines him, George uses mind power to move a pencil across the desk. He senses when earthquakes are coming and locates a lost boy by clairvoyantly discerning the child's whereabouts.

How does he do it? "We're all made of the same stuff, energy," George explains to the curious who inquire about his abilities. "The energy in me is in partnership with the energy [in the objects]." With all the hubris of the Scientology and parapsychology advocate that he is, Travolta speaks through George to declare, "I am what everyone can be. I'm a possibility. The human spirit is the voyage, that's the expedition."

Such occult irrationalism is a staple of the New Age movement, which links paranormal practitioners and extraterrestrial fans.

The New Age Connection

Even the most cursory analysis of UFO encounters suggests that the message carried from out there to down here is consistent with an occult/metaphysical view of cosmology. As I have already mentioned, studies show that those who experience UFO encounters believed in extraterrestrials before their experience. In addition, most UFO contactees and abductees were already involved in some form of occult practice or psychic experimentation prior to their initial encounter with aliens.

After prolonged study of alien contacts and abduction accounts, I have distilled the essence of these experiences with these aliens, and the themes they convey, into the following New Age propositions:

NUMBER ONE: ALIEN MANIPULATION

Out of the hundreds of accounts I have researched, including firsthand interviews, none of the victims has expressed any sense of solace about his or her extraterrestrial rendezvous. Aliens offer no peace of mind. Instead, psychiatrists who have studied the abduction phenomenon say most encounters result in severe trauma, followed by anxiety-ridden nightmares and frightening flashbacks. This initial reaction of terror finally gave way to resignation when the contactee submitted to being a vessel for further extradimensional communication. These people felt like manipulated robots, with little choice but to obey the more highly evolved beings.

If not possessed by these entities, the contactees at least felt controlled to the point of having no further life of their own. Every decision in their lives became contingent on the higher calling of the aliens. If these messengers meant well, and they were as spiritually advanced as they generally claimed to be, why wasn't their visitation more comforting?

NUMBER TWO: COSMIC AWARENESS

The theme of cosmic awareness is universal in tales of alien abduction. Cosmic consciousness is what matters, according to the aliens, not any private or solitary goals of the person involved. And since the contactee has allegedly not yet evolved to the degree of spiritual advancement of the aliens, the earthbound human must concede any spiritual opinion to this cosmic wisdom.

This theme of alien wisdom is similar to the ideas put forth by the occult-obsessed disciple of Freud, Carl Jung. The Swiss psychologist theorized that all people can tap into what he called the collective unconscious. According to Jung, there is an area of our unconscious that contains information derived from the experiences of the human race as a whole, rather than those of the individual. This storehouse contains universal symbols called archetypes, which present themselves spontaneously in dreams or visions, evoking strong imaginative responses.

As a student of Eastern mystical thought, Jung saw its connection with the UFO phenomenon. He noted the Tibetan Buddhist concept of the mandala, a disk-shaped symbol used for meditation, which signifies totality. The flying saucers might not be real objects, Jung suggested, but rather mandalas, which people who yearn for harmony and equilibrium visualize in the sky. Such subjective notions of spiritual universality (which are very near to the Hindu idea of Brahmanistic oneness) are contrary to the biblical worldview of objective truth embodied in the person of Christ and revealed through His words in holy Scripture.

NUMBER THREE: SPIRITUAL TRANSCENDENCE

Aliens expound the common occult idea of upward transcendence to higher spiritual planes. There is no ultimate truth, only an ever-expanding awareness of progressive revelation. To acquire this spiritual knowledge, aliens tell their pupils to look to their "higher selves."

Unlike biblical Christianity, which teaches that truth is an absolute (John 14:6), aliens usually say that it has taken them many epochs to evolve into their exalted spiritual status. They invite earthlings to join them in this journey toward an elevated consciousness by exploring psychic inner awareness.

NUMBER FOUR: IMPENDING ENVIRONMENTAL DISASTERS

Some aliens say that their visits are for the purpose of monitoring our biosphere, and that we have endangered our species. They warn of coming global cataclysms unless we reverse our neglect of the environment. But don't worry. Our benevolent buddies from outer space have arrived in the nick of time to avert disaster.

Sounding like poster people for the Sierra Club or Greenpeace, extraterrestrials preach a gospel of environmental pantheism. Their ecological sermon is rooted in an animistic view of the Earth as a living organism, also called the Gaia hypothesis. Man is the master of Earth's fate if he is willing to worship Mother Nature to the point of treating the rivers and trees as spirit entities. There is no room for a divine Creator in this worldview.

NUMBER FIVE: PSYCHIC INVOLVEMENT

Because most aliens communicate by mental telepathy, all paranormal practices are deemed harmless. Like Spielberg's

E. T., who floated objects and supernaturally healed wounds, the aliens contacting humankind invite us to participate in a panoply of occult acts.

These space visitors recommend astral projection (out-of-body experiences) as a way to release ourselves from the confines of Earth's gravity and visit other dimensional realities. Some aliens even suggest that their ability to circumvent normal time-space limitations is the result of spirit travel.

Automatic writing, the psychomotor manipulation of one's hands and fingers without conscious effort, is one way such beings may choose to communicate. An alien, claiming to be sent by Christ, is supposed to have communicated the quasi-Christian metaphysical book, *A Course in Miracles*, through automatic writing.

To aliens, psychic powers have nothing to do with demons or illusion. They explain that the paranormal is just another realm of reality, quite normal to them because of their spiritually advanced state. To experience the universe as aliens perceive it, abductees are encouraged to return to Earth and raise their level of ethereal awareness by exploring acts of divination and prognostication.

NUMBER SIX: AVOIDANCE OF BIBLICAL THEMES

Aliens may say they have made contact with humans to demonstrate unconditional love, but they never mention the biblical themes of sin, judgment, and forgiveness. They do not see man's moral predicament as resulting from original sin but from his failure to explore his inherent, but dormant, spiritual capacities.

The cult of Scientology, for example, teaches that mankind is descended from a race of omnipotent gods called thetans. These outer-space aliens gave up their powers to enter the Material-Energy-Space-Time (referred to as MEST) world of

Earth. By reincarnation they evolved upward to become humans who could not remember their former deified state. Thus, Scientologists are encouraged to awaken their thetan potential by removing all mental blocks called *engrams,* emotional hangups stored in the subconscious.

New Agers often refer to Christ, but only in gratuitous terms. The Lord is never worshiped, He is only admired as one of many ascended spiritual adepts. The Bible is just one among many sacred writings. What these New Agers believe is similar to what aliens tell abductees.

NUMBER SEVEN: DENIAL OF THE INCARNATION

Aliens either ignore the redemption of Christ on the cross or openly deny it. To them Christ is not the God-man, the only Mediator between man and God (1 Tim. 2:5). In extraterrestrial theology, Jesus Christ is relegated to a minor figure in the pantheon of those who have heeded the message to follow an inner truth and acquire spiritual awareness, the Christ-consciousness available to all who follow the aliens' advice. Sometimes Jesus is even considered to be an advanced alien who ended up with his own galaxy to rule.

This is the theory of the Urantia cult. The 2,097-page *Urantia Book* claims to have been delivered by extraterrestrial beings. Its pages say it is the "finest major divine revelation since the coming of Christ to our planet." Urantia proposes a new understanding of man's evolutionary ascent, which is based on the perspective of beings from another world. Our universe is divided into Earth (Urantia as it's known by these extraterrestrials) and its superuniverse, Havona. Urantia (Earth) is part of a local universe of ten million inhabitable worlds, known as Nebadon. Jesus was actually the earthly incarnation of an alien called Michael of Nebadon.

Jesus, by Urantia calculation, is *a son* of God who perfected his divinity by seven incarnations among various creatures of the universe. His seventh incarnation on Urantia in the person of Joshua ben Joseph was intended to teach us that we are all sons of God. Man, according to Urantia, is not a unique creation of God but an evolving being, destined to be an angelic spirit and, eventually, a god.

NUMBER EIGHT: ALIEN ATTACKS ON SCRIPTURE

The recommended reading list of UFO occupants almost never includes the Word of God. When the Bible is referred to, it is said to be merely a good book that should be augmented by superior, newer revelations. Some aliens even go so far as to say that the Bible is the enemy of spiritual advancement because of its chauvinistic and anti-intellectual bias.

Aliens also part ways with Scripture over the issue of evolution. Since accepting the existence of aliens is based on evolutionary advancement and the theory of life arising spontaneously on any planet where conditions permit, the uniqueness of the Garden of Eden story must be dismissed. Therefore, aliens may quote the Bible to contactees—but only when it suits their purpose.

NUMBER NINE: ALIEN EXCLUSIVITY

Aliens do not like to be ignored. In their cosmological scheme, there is only one way to interpret reality: their way! While they may appear benevolent in their intent to aid earthlings through the coming apocalypse, the only true way out of this annihilation is by following their plan. This arrogance is similar to the New Age's underlying exclusivity.

New Agers, who are fond of touting their acceptance of *all* religious paths and spiritual experiences, proclaim a universality of consciousness that recognizes any traditional or shamanistic pathway to God at the same time they reject the conservative, evangelical approach to spirituality. To the New Age, Christ is okay as long as He is one of many masters, but never the supreme embodiment of Truth.

NUMBER TEN: ANGELIC ASSOCIATION

The current angel-crazy faction of the New Age movement is partially an outgrowth of equating UFO occupants with the heavenly messengers of the Bible. In fact, some aliens say that the Old and New Testament stories of angelic intervention are really tales of extraterrestrial visitations. The examples they give range from the angels who called on Lot before the destruction of Sodom to the angel who warned Christ's earthly father, Joseph, to flee to Egypt.

This contention loses credibility when compared to the true scriptural account of the purpose of angelic visitations. In God's Word angels always carry out a specific mission as the result of His divine directive. In Luke 2:9–14 they announce the birth of Christ and convey God's glorious revelation of salvation for the ages. In 2 Chronicles 20:22 they execute the Lord's wrath and judgment in the destruction of Jehoshaphat's enemies. In Genesis 19:13 they predict the overthrow of Gomorrah. Unlike UFO aliens, these angels of the Lord never draw attention to themselves; instead they direct man's attention heavenward to the God of the Bible. And their message never supports occult practices.

In short, the New Age nuttiness of the aliens' message is proof that these extraterrestrials are opposed to biblical Christianity. Their gospel is surely the doctrine of demons, which the Bible says will be taught in the last days (1 Tim. 4:1).

Indeed there is even a millennial component to the aliens' message, which should not be surprising with the year 2000 approaching. Occultists of all sorts have the feeling that at the start of another thousand-year cycle mankind is going to take some kind of leap of cosmic consciousness. But Judgment Day eschatology (the belief in prophecies of catastrophic events resulting from God's wrath) is not in this picture. Instead little gray men with a message of peace descend from a hovering spacecraft to save mankind.

Many gullible adherents of the alien messengers trust the extraterrestrials' statement that mankind's vibrational rate is about to be changed by an upward shift in spiritual consciousness. The aliens say they will lead the way. To prepare their followers for this momentous occasion, the space visitors encourage them to cultivate their inherent psychic powers.

Extrasensory Deception

The basic premise of the paranormal is that unexplained phenomena, which defy the laws of the universe, are the manifestation of untapped powers of the human soul. The corollary of that premise is that anyone can tap into this unleashed potential if he or she is willing to set aside all cultural conventions, rational objections, and religious inhibitions.

In the eighties New Agers were busy channeling the spirits of Ramtha and a host of other entities. Today their attention has turned to more practical applications. One New Age spiritist claims she transforms her boardrooms into Ouija-boardrooms. "I'll be sitting in a meeting and a vapor-like apparition will come out of people and tell me what's really going on in that meeting."[1]

What other paranormal practices are popular today? Some seek the consciousness-raising teachings of the Armenian mystic G. I. Gurdjieff. Since his death in 1949, Gurdjieff's fame has steadily increased through the devotion of secret so-called G-O groups. Gurdjieff's blend of Asian occultism and mystical Christianity fits well with today's paranormal curiosity. The basic tenet is that man's consciousness is open to higher planes of awareness, though most are spiritually asleep to this possibility. This quest for self-knowledge is typical of many of today's gnostic-based cults who see no need to believe in God if they can develop supernatural powers of their own.

Shamanistic journeying is another fashionable way to leave behind the mundane tasks of life's daily grind. Through meditation and trance states the mental explorer can enter an alpha state, which some refer to as "brain-wave surfing." In this altered state of consciousness practitioners can contact and enhance the supposed pure inner state of humanity. They then try to draw this essence into their daily lives to relieve stress and alter reality. This touring of the soul is so popular that *The Utne Reader,* a countercultural digest of hip fads, sponsored a "Living Theater of the Soul," a kind of paranormal road show.

"I want to believe" is the mantra of this popular paranormal movement of neospiritualists. For those fed up with conventional Christianity, the pursuit of the paranormal has become a religion. And if you've already got a religion, that's okay. Just tack on a copy of *The Celestine Prophecy* or travel to Sedona, Arizona, and chant inside an Indian medicine wheel. Adding a little religion to your life is good, because it shows a predisposition to the spiritual realm.

PSYCHIC PHENOMENA

What are these supposedly inherent paranormal powers advocated by the aliens? The term *psi* is an abbreviation for all psychic phenomena and extrasensory curiosities. Specifically they include the following:

Aura Reading: Perceiving the emanations of color surrounding the human body to determine the condition of the body, soul, and spirit.

The colors, which radiate a few inches to several feet in all directions, are said to be a manifestation of one's higher self. Psychics say anyone can read these auras if he or she is tuned in to them. The dominant color radiating at any time indicates the person's physical, emotional, or spiritual condition.

Clairvoyance: Receiving information from an object or event by nonsensory means.

This knowledge may be about the past, present, or future. For example, a psychic may hold the personal effect (a ring, a watch, a piece of clothing) of a missing person and claim to know his or her whereabouts.

ESP: Extrasensory perception, the ability to perceive beyond the capability of the five natural senses.

This discernment may be by clairvoyance (see above) or telepathy (see below). Cognitive forms of ESP operate in the realm of postcognition (consciousness of events in the past), cognition (knowledge about the present), and precognition (predictions concerning the future).

Psychokinesis: Affecting an object, event, or situation by mental powers.

Known as PK for short, this paranormal discipline involves exerting psychic powers on an outside goal. This is done without the exertion of muscles or physical energy or the use of instruments. It is popularly displayed in such theatrical tricks as spoon bending, table tipping, and levitation.

Psychometry: Receiving paranormal information from an object.

This a specific form of clairvoyance that operates by the psychic receiving vibrations from the object in question.

Remote Viewing: Discerning something across a distance without the psychic's direct physical contact with the person, object, or circumstance.

Psychics often use this aspect of the paranormal to send healing to someone at another location. Some spiritualists claim the ability to discern the form of certain shapes and symbols at a distant site by mental impression.

Telepathy: Discerning another person's mental state or transmitting thoughts to another person.

This communication occurs mind-to-mind. It may occur spontaneously or as the result of a deliberate attempt to invade someone else's consciousness.

Out-of-body experiences, moving objects by mental projections, levitation, clairvoyance, ESP, and telepathy are all occult practices which are popular in the New Age movement. They all involve some sort of supernatural assistance. And they are all advocated by extraterrestrials.

Many people ask me whether these paranormal pursuits are good, evil, or morally neutral. They want to know if the encouragement of extraterrestrials to explore the nonrational is a blessing or a bane.

I believe we must search Scripture to see if such occurrences are forbidden. Then the psychic ability must be subjected to the authority of Christ and compelled to cease if it is not from Him. Finally we must examine its purpose: does it truly exalt the Lord? Remember, any supernatural occurrence receives its power from one of two possible sources: God or the devil (via Satan's demons).

Those who pursue the paranormal usually dismiss the idea that such things could come from evil since some psychics, such as those who aid police investigators in solving crimes, appear to do good. But should these honorable works be construed as indicating that clairvoyance can be blessed by God?

Christ addressed this issue in Matthew 7:22–23. He warned that on Judgment Day some will say they did great things, even in the name of Christ. The Lord's response will be: "I never knew you; depart from Me."

A display of the paranormal by a well-meaning individual is not necessarily a measure of divine endorsement. Acts 10:38 speaks of the miracles Christ performed and adds the qualification, "God was with Him." There can be no exception to this rule for anyone who claims the power to perform the paranormal.

The attraction of the paranormal is not godly. It is rooted in Satan's appeal to Adam and Eve: "You will be like God." Selfishness and spiritual rebellion are the true reasons people turn to psychic phenomena. Instead of surrendering to God's purpose and trusting in Him with all their hearts (Prov. 3:5–6), they want to be "like God" and chart their own paths.

A high percentage of those who claim to have been abducted by aliens say they were told that the mission of extraterrestrials is to help mankind ascend to become gods. Should that manifesto be acclaimed? No. Nowhere does the Bible tell us that our eternal destiny is godhood. Instead our purpose throughout the ages will be to worship God and declare His glory (Rev. 7:9–10).

We need to be careful not to be tricked by the deceptive message delivered by so-called extraterrestrials; it is too easy to be lulled by nice-sounding phrases. That's why the biblical test of 1 Thessalonians 5:21 cannot be ignored: "Test all things; hold fast what is good."

God's view of prognosticative error was so stern that the Hebrew people instituted capital punishment for any prophet whose prophecies did not come true. The reason the Bible has such exacting standards is that psychic fatalism lures people away from trusting God. Even more dangerous is the possibility that volitional responsibility may be ignored.

Those who follow the doctrines of alien messengers may claim the excuse that someone out there told them what to do. This self-deception is the ultimate end of all who seek the assistance of aliens. Paul warned the Galatians, "But even if we, or an angel from heaven [*or an extraterrestrial*], preach any other gospel to you than what we have preached to you, let him be accursed" (Gal. 1:8).

In spite of the biblical warning, our national obsession for communication with alien messengers and space visitors continues unabated—and the American government has spent over $60 million of the taxpayers' money trying to tune in the extraterrestrial signals.

PART 2

Who
Are
They?

CHAPTER SIX

Seeking Extraterrestrial Signals

If E. T. is talking, America is listening. NASA's Search for Extraterrestrial Intelligence (SETI) did its job for more than a decade, and private researchers are still at it—but so far no one has phoned home. Undaunted, the NASA project's first director, Bernard Oliver, says he is proud of the job he has done to determine "whether we are alone as an intelligent species in the universe, or whether there are others." Without any deference to the religious component of such a serious search, he adds, "Modern astronomy and biology predict that life is very common."[1]

The search for an extraterrestrial message began in the 1960s when radio astronomers around the world listened to various microwave frequencies but had no success contacting anyone or anything. NASA began its SETI project in the late seventies, using computer-monitored radio telescopes at the Ames Research Center in Mountain View, California, to scan the skies for extraterrestrial signals. Other giant listening devices were operated at the Goldstone Deep Space Communications Complex in the Mojave Desert and at Arecibo, Puerto Rico. NASA telescopes tracked a particular star for five- to fifteen-minute intervals at a particular frequency. The list of possible star targets that might be orbited by life-supporting planets includes about one thousand sun-like stars, from four to one hundred light years away.

Then in 1983 the Planetary Society, headed by the late science guru Carl Sagan, launched Project Sentinel with a rented radio telescope from Harvard University. That effort eventually expanded its search to 8.4 million microwave channels at frequencies from about 1,000 to 10,000 megahertz. Spurred by the prospect of using supercomputers capable of searches ten billion times more intense, NASA launched a new $100 million, ten-year project in 1992.

But even with casting the net that wide, no signal from out there has reached us yet. If it should, though, NASA's Bernard Oliver does not think the public would be surprised. He says, "A lot of people are prepared for it. They've watched so much science fiction."[2]

In 1993 Congress pulled the plug on NASA's new Targeted Search project. After spending more than $60 million on the original decade-long SETI research, a new crop of conservative legislators were not willing to continue spending $10 million per year to search for civilizations in outer space.

If E. T. still wants to phone home, it now looks like he will have to call collect.

BETTING ON THE EXTRATERRESTRIAL ODDS

Enthusiasts who expect to find intelligent life in outer space, however, have not given up. The search for extraterrestrial signals is now carried on by the SETI Institute, a nonprofit organization which operates Project Phoenix, a privately funded continuation of NASA's Targeted Search.

Current SETI Institute president, astronomer Frank Drake, was thrilled when the so-called Martian rocks yielded what were interpreted as microbes. "It confirms what we've always believed—that life arises wherever the conditions are right."[3]

The SETI search is based on a purely statistical bet on the odds: Because our sun is just one star in a galaxy of 150 billion stars, in a universe of billions of galaxies, the universe *must* be teeming with life. And some of it just has to be intelligent. "We are just one iota among countless iotas in the universe," SETI astronomer Drake insists.[4]

Is that the only motive compelling us to communicate with extraterrestrials? Or could there be another, unspoken agenda that invokes a latent but more spiritually coercive drive to contact whoever or whatever is in outer space?

SETI Spiritualism

To most people, the biblical injunction of Leviticus 19:31, "Give no regard to mediums and familiar spirits; do not seek after them, to be defiled by them: I am the LORD your God," is outdated. This prohibition against contact with evil forces is considered the archaic taboo of an ancient nomadic tribe with no relevance for today.

But for Christians who believe the Word of God is an unchanging rule of faith, this warning against communication with demons is as meaningful today as when it was given. Let me point out three quotes by those with an interest in UFOs and show the modern-day application of Leviticus 19:31.

SCIENTIFIC SPIRITUALISM IN ACTION

First, consider a comment made by the current director of SETI Institute's Project Phoenix, Dr. Jill Tarter. With a touch of scientific arrogance, Dr. Tarter says, "We've asked the priests . . . our sources of wisdom in the past (about extraterrestrial life). Now the thing to do is ask the engineers and scientists if they can get verifiable, concrete evidence." In an even more telling comment, Dr. Tarter described the SETI effort as a "real leap of faith."[5]

Note Dr. Tarter's disdain for religious explanations of life in the universe. Then, in contrast, she refers to the use of radio telescopes to eavesdrop on stellar civilizations as a "leap of faith." In other words, this SETI research director is unwilling to trust biblical edicts regarding life's origins, but she eagerly places her trust in hoped-for microwave transmissions from unidentified extraterrestrial sources. In doing so, she has exchanged the tenets of Christianity for the suppositions of science.

The second comment I found interesting came from Professor Leo Sprinkle, former director of the University of Wyoming Division of Counseling and Testing. Dr. Sprinkle, an avid devotee of abduction accounts and a consultant for the Aerial Phenomenon Research Organization, has hypnotized dozens of people who say they have been aboard UFOs. Professor Sprinkle says, "My guess is that they (UFOs) are more than a physical phenomenon. They're a psychic or spiritual phenomenon."

Here we see the setting aside of scientific logic, by a trained psychologist, in favor of an occult explanation. Sprinkle's "proof" regarding the source of UFOs is the highly questionable practice of regressive hypnotherapy. This academician puts his trust in the information provided by self-proclaimed contactees who have been subjected to a trance state!

Consider yet another revealing comment from the late Dr. J. Allen Hynek who, until his death, was the world's ranking authority on UFOs. Hynek once said, "I suspect that a very advanced civilization might know something about the connection between mind and matter that we don't."

Here again we have an eminent scientist offering a metaphysical observation of UFOs. Hynek makes two essentially spiritual assumptions. First, he concludes that any other civilization that exists must be more advanced. Hence, any contacts they make with us would place us in a subservient position to their superior intelligence regarding matters of fact and faith. Second, Hynek endorses the concept of a mind-matter connection. This is an occult notion that seeks to disguise the work of demons in the realm of extraterrestrials as some natural but inexplicable phenomenon, which man must be unafraid to investigate.

Hynek eventually abandoned the "nuts and bolts" theory of UFOs—the notion that they are actual spacecraft piloted by technologically advanced aliens. In 1976 he said, "There are just too many things going against this theory. To me, it seems ridiculous that super intelligence would travel great distances to do relatively stupid things like stop cars, collect soil samples, and frighten people."[6] After thirty years of serious UFO research, Hynek finally adopted the theory that UFOs are from another dimension, or a parallel reality.

Yet, as far as I know, Hynek never rejected the possibility of advanced civilizations existing somewhere in the universe; he simply was forced to admit, as an empirical scientist, that he had seen no concrete proof of these supposedly advanced aliens.

A SLIPPERY SLOPE

Now that we see the dangerous slippery slope of spiritualism that Tarter, Sprinkle, Hynek, and other ufologists are on, let me explain how this relates to the ban on witchcraft activity that God pronounced in Leviticus 19:31.

First, let us consider the terms that Scripture uses in regard to spiritualism. Mediums (known as channelers in the New Age movement) are individuals who give their wills to demons so that these unseen spiritual forces can use their faculties to communicate from the spirit world. In the case of necromancy, the demons imitate dead human beings. These evil spirits are referred to as "familiar" spirits, so-called because the medium often yields to them and thus is familiar with their presence and manner of manifestation. In addition to impersonating the dead, the familiar spirits of mediums may also make predictions, give advice, and promulgate false doctrine.

The most vivid biblical example of this form of spiritualism is found in 1 Samuel 28, which describes the visit of King Saul to the witch of En Dor. Saul sought the advice of the dead prophet Samuel and asked the witch to conjure him. A demon masquerading as the late prophet mimicked Samuel so well that the witch responded as if she really believed it was the dead man returned alive. (Some Bible scholars believe that Samuel actually did show up at the séance; that interpretation is a possible explanation for what happened, but it's not necessary to settle that debate in this book.)

God so sternly judged Saul's disobedience in consulting a medium that it cost him his life! First Chronicles 10:13 says, "So Saul died for his unfaithfulness which he had committed against the LORD, because he did not keep the word of the LORD, and also because he consulted a medium for guidance."

Why is the sin of seeking a medium so serious in the eyes

of God? Turning to witchcraft (consulting mediums and familiar spirits) is seeking to look beyond the veil, which shields the unknown, to discover knowledge providentially hidden. In doing so, the seeker disregards the will and wisdom of the Lord and rejects His authority. The real sin is the solicitor's denial of God's supremacy by going outside of the boundaries God has established to engage in an act of willful disobedience.

Tarter, Sprinkle, and Hynek are guilty of this transgression. Their "leap of faith" to inquire into a "spiritual phenomenon" without biblical guidelines leaves them open to demonic deception. This bold substitution of spiritualism for science is a form of mediumship. Just as the Greek citizens of Athens built their altar to the unknown god (Acts 17:23), the likes of Tarter and others erect giant dish antennas to probe the heavens in search of some distant trace of life, indicated by pulsing microwaves.

These scientists disregard what the Bible says about the uniqueness of life on Earth and seek contact with advanced beings beyond the stars. In my opinion, they are seekers of the occult. Their radio telescopes are "mediums" and the interstellar source they seek is the realm of familiar spirits. I predict that eventually they *will* receive some kind of message, and that these "voices" will be heralded as the guides into a new age of human spiritual potential.

There are other ways of discovering alien life, besides searching the skies with telescopes. One way is to interpret unusual occurrences on Earth as evidence that aliens are among us. Other UFO enthusiasts cite crop circles as one proof of alien existence.

Crop Circles

Certain farmers from more than thirty countries, including Japan, Canada, the former Soviet Union, New Zealand, and

England, think they have made extraterrestrial contact. These farmers suggest we turn off those telescopes and save the money. They believe that extraterrestrials are creating crop circles as their way of saying, "We're here and we're flattening your fields."

This peculiar sensation started in the farmlands of southern England in the mid-1970s. Strange circular depressions up to ten feet in diameter appeared in grain fields, leaving no clues how they got there. These puzzling circles—large sweeping areas neatly flattened in a swirling pattern—do not exhibit the kind of rough damage caused by harsh weather or animals. Though some farmers tried to cash in on the phenomenon by perpetrating hoaxes, most researchers could find no man-made explanation for the occurrences. A new scientific discipline emerged to study the phenomenon: cereology.

Crop circles have been around since the Middle Ages, but their frequency has increased dramatically in this century. The first modern-day sighting was in 1976 when a farm worker at Headbourne Worthy in Hampshire, England, noticed a large circular pattern in a field near the A34 highway. Since then, people have reported nearly one thousand occurrences each year worldwide. Whoever or whatever has been flattening the fields seems to have concentrated on the United Kingdom; some say it's because this area is home to the mysterious occult stone formations of Stonehenge.

But crop circles have also appeared in the United States.

In South Dakota a farmer discovered an eighty-foot-long backward question mark swirled in his wheat field. A hoax? As the representative of the Mutual UFO Network (MUFON), an international organization of UFO watchers put it, "There are no hoaxers in South Dakota. These are hardworking farmers. They don't have time for nonsense like messing up their fields."[7]

Apparently crops are not the only target for circles. A rural

British Columbia family found a thirty-nine-foot ring dug in their driveway. Later that night the family saw a cone of red light over an apple tree. The next day, every apple was gone.

What intrigues those who study crop circles is the beautiful geometric formations that level fields in a precise pattern. The plant, usually a grain, is flattened within two inches of the ground in a distinctive swirl. Strangely the stalk is not severed and continues to ripen until harvest. The formations range from single rings to more complex quintuplets and even a so-called "Celtic cross" of four circles linked by one large ring. From there the designs get more complex with some swirls in opposite directions and also a single circle with a long curling tail. Others have surreal patterns—test tubes, dumbbells, keys. The circles range in size from a tire to a football field. Most mysteriously, investigators seldom see any sign of human footprints, tire tracks, or any evidence of human intervention.

Meanwhile, the fascination with crop circles means big business. Shutterbugs snap away and flying helicopters charge $20 a head to fly viewers over the scene. For the serious aficionado there are balloon rides and trips aboard microlight aircraft for lingering aerial views of the circles. And don't forget to pick up a $10 Mystery Circle T-shirt before you leave!

What causes these circles? Dust devils or low swirling winds, as some have suggested? Oversized grasshoppers, fairies, amorous deer, or crazed hedgehogs? What about the accompanying occurrences: apples in an orchard all falling to the ground at the same time; corn disappearing, but husks remaining in place? Could it be that extraterrestrials are exploring our food sources?

Some scientists have given natural explanations. Others cite paranormal phenomena. And still others claim crop circles are hoaxes. Let's look at each explanation.

IS THERE A SCIENTIFIC EXPLANATION?

One scientist speculates that a "plasma vortex phenomenon," a previously nonexistent form of atmospheric disturbance associated with electrical effects, is the culprit. The plasma effect is claimed to be a "spinning ball of air" highly charged with electricity, which has flattened the crop fields.[8] But what cannot be explained is how a vicious wind could sculpt such intricate creations in a relatively small area.

A team of Japanese scientists, led by physicist Yoshi-Hiko Ohtsuki, joined the search for an explanation. Ohtsuki postulated that ball lightning generated by microwaves in the atmosphere flattened the crops; he created crop-like circular patterns both in the laboratory and on a computer programmed to simulate balls of highly charged lightning. Ohtsuki's work was so impressive that the British journal *Nature* published his findings, leading some to conclude the mystery was solved.[9]

Other people in search of an answer have turned to the paranormal.

IS THE EXPLANATION PARANORMAL?

Understandably, UFOs come up often as a way to explain these strange patterns. According to one theory from the U.K., the landing pods of huge mother ships laid the crops low as they visited nearby Stonehenge. The UFOs were drawn to the spot by the fabled psychic powers of the ancient stone monuments. Some psychic investigators had the idea that UFOs were trying to leave messages.

At least one Canadian farmer claims to have seen the culprits, and they were UFOs. Edwin Fuhr was riding on his plow when he looked up and noticed five shiny, saucer-like objects spinning eighteen inches off the ground. He watched them for two hours until they finally departed, leaving behind five flattened crop circles in their wake.

ARE CROP CIRCLES HOAXES?

Several years ago two men, David Chorley, sixty-two, and Douglas Bower, sixty-seven, came forward to say they were behind the U.K. crop circles. They had been sneaking around southern England for thirteen years, they claimed, fashioning twenty-five to thirty circles each growing season. The duo suggested their actions inspired copycats all over the world who apparently figured out their method of deception.

How did David and Douglas do it? In quite an unsophisticated way.

The hoaxers made a scale drawing of the intended patterns. Then Chorley and Bower went to a wheat field with their equipment: a four-foot-long wooden plank, a ball of string, and a baseball cap with a wire threaded through the visor as a sighting device. At the center of the intended site, Bower held one end of the string. The other end was attached to the plank, held horizontally at knee level by Chorley. He circled around Bower, pushing the grain gently forward. With perseverance, and a sense of humor, the two landscape artists say they fooled millions for years.

Other experts on the issue say, "Whoa, not so fast." Perhaps the story of the hoax is a hoax itself. What about the circles in the U.S., Canada, and elsewhere? Also, when Chorley and Bower were asked by the press to demonstrate their art, the circle they formed was far less true than the ones seen elsewhere in Hampshire and Wiltshire. In addition, the plant stems were broken and ragged, unlike previously flattened fields.

One of the detractors is Dr. Terry Meaden, formerly associate professor of physics at Dalhousie University, Halifax,

Nova Scotia. Meaden heads the crop circle study group, CERES (Circle Effect Research, with the ES added to the acronym in honor of the Roman goddess of agriculture). He says that proof exists for the theory of circles caused by eddies of wind running along hillsides. In defense of continuing investigation, Meaden declared, "I have no doubt that Bower and Chorley are responsible for some hoaxes. We have seen an increasing number of improbable circles in recent years which were obviously not genuine because of the amount of damage done to the crops."[10]

What about other strange events inside the circles? Supposedly, investigators found electronic signals emitting from the ground. Compasses mysteriously twirled and dowsing rods vibrated and then crossed. Cameras imploded. A Japanese television crew, which spent months studying crop circles, lost several cameras to the phenomenon. An engineer also pointed out that a crystal pendant on a string spun slowly clockwise when suspended at the center of the circles.

What is to be made of all this? Certainly some circles are the work of hoaxers who somehow concealed their footprints. If that's the entire explanation, though, what a revealing insight it is into mankind's gullibility. Scientists, grounded in a naturalistic approach to understanding all inexplicable occurrences, were fooled for more than a decade by two eccentric senior-citizen pranksters. Leaders of academia ignored evidence in favor of the assumption that no intelligence created the circles and the cause must therefore be atmospheric. On the other hand, equally astute investigators assumed that ET intelligence did it and looked for paranormal confirmation by swinging crystals!

If hoaxers were responsible, both the naturalists and the UFO occultists missed the point. Both saw the circles and denied reality to accommodate their own worldview. If such learned people reached such wrong conclusions for so long, why should we trust the intellectuals and scientists of our age when it comes to determining the origins of life? If their biases intrude on something as simple as crop circles, can we expect them to be any more accurate when probing the geological past?

Furthermore, if there is any supernaturalism attached to the forming of some circles, which of the investigators can be trusted? The natural scientist too quickly explains away any evidence that is contrary to a physical cause. The occult investigator also ignores any evil supernatural intent in favor of a benevolent extraterrestrial source.

My twenty-plus years of observing the operations of the occult and dealing with supernatural demonic forces has led me to conclude that phenomena like crop circles generally have a supernatural explanation. I believe the powers of evil lurk behind some of these occurrences.

SATAN, THE EXPLOITER

Satan is an imitator, not an originator. Frankly, he is too slothful to think up new ways to tempt and deceive humanity. Why should he? The old ways have sufficed for six thousand years. Thus, when something happens with the potential for occult deception, the devil is seldom the creator. He exploits what already is and transforms it into something it is not.

When Satan spots something in human experience that draws man away from God, he often capitalizes on the circumstance. For example, the devil may not have "invented" the first Ouija board; the fallen, sinful curiosity of man may have simply sought some device to communicate with the unknown. But the devil was quick to see the evil potential of such a diversion and then added his influence.

My guess is that humans formed the first crop circles, just as many charlatan psychics employ purely natural tricks to deceive those who follow them. It took Chorley and Bower thirteen years to reveal their prank. Will time reveal that others manufactured similar incidents? Probably. But it would be a mistake to take a purely naturalistic approach and assume that every circle was a hoax.

When the devil saw that the circles were a clever way to draw attention to the paranormal, he sent demons to help do what man had started. That's why the crystal spun, why radio waves were detected, and why some say they actually saw UFOs near the circle sites.

The tragedy of our hour is that neither the gullible occultist nor the atheistic scientist has answers for the unsolved mysteries of our generation. Both are caught in the same devil's web, where facts are manipulated and logic is suspended. These are surely the End Times when the great delusion spoken of in 2 Thessalonians 2:11 has begun to grip those minds not surrendered to Christ's authority. The enigma of what is being done by alien forces out there, and down here, can only be truthfully resolved by Christians who possess the discipline of intellectual acumen and the humility of biblical obedience.

And the need for spiritual discernment, based in a thorough understanding of God's Word, has never been greater, for the tales of alien involvement with humanity grow ever more bizarre—and so do the shameless Scripture-twisting tactics of these "enlightened beings." Some even say they are here on Earth to encourage people to let aliens walk into their bodies. Let's hear what one of these "walk-ins" has to say.

CHAPTER SEVEN

Aliens Among Us: Abductions and Walk-ins

For forty years sighters of UFOs have been warning us that aliens are about to land en masse and take over our minds, if not our shopping malls. But what is unique today is that this fascination with paranormal phenomena has become a national pastime. Ever since Americans fell for Steven Spielberg's lovable E. T., our society has been obsessed with aliens and things extraterrestrial.

But those who claim to be from outer space are often not what they seem, as I found out one day when I interviewed a couple of so-called aliens on my nationally syndicated radio program.

The Walk-ins

Several years ago, I invited two of the strangest guests I've ever hosted to join me on a broadcast. Frederick von Mierers, a top-rated fashion model, and his male companion, John Andreadis, had been featured in psychic Ruth Montgomery's book *Aliens Among Us*.

Spirit guides told Montgomery that the star Arcturus, one of the brightest of the northern hemisphere in the constellation Boötes, was the home of spiritually advanced beings who had returned to earthly bodies for the good of humanity. They were "walk-ins," aliens who took over earthly bodies. These men were not only guests on my radio program, but claimed they were also guests on planet Earth. My talk show audience was stunned by their preposterous claims.

Frederick's tone was coldly serious as he told me directly, "I am the reincarnation of Jeremiah of the Old Testament, and in January of 1978 I came directly from Arcturus and walked into the body in which I now dwell.

"I saw myself buried alive in an Egyptian sarcophagus and was initiated as a high priest in Egypt. Over a period of seven days, three beings materialized to me and taught me the secrets of Hindu astrology. It was then that I knew the body I lived in was that of Frederick von Mierers, but my consciousness was that of the hydrogen-light body I left behind in Arcturus."

Frederick's friend John chimed in. "In former lives both of us were adepts in ancient India. We helped to plan and erect the great pyramid of Giza. We have accomplished great things on Earth because we come from a planet that is without atmosphere and thus is a perfect environment for soul improvement."

As unbelievable as their stories were, their claim of a spiritual mission was most incredible. "I have come to encourage people to allow aliens to walk into their bodies," Frederick said. "This is the way they can come back to

Christ-consciousness and speed up their karma. Once walk-ins have taken over enough bodies, the evil forces lingering from the dark side of Atlantis will change the energy of world leaders so they understand unconditional love for all beings."

How long does it take for a walk-in to occur? Seventeen years was the answer.

Any advice for those anticipating a walk-in? It's best to be a vegetarian.

Any imperatives for encouraging this to happen? About the year 2000 the Earth will shift on its axis and the New Age will dawn.

Frederick's sermon was simple: "Space beings, souls like us, inhabit thought-worlds and desire to incarnate by walking into full-grown bodies. They are beamed down from space-ships, which are thought-ships that materialize as they enter Earth's dimension.

"Anyone who can grasp this can be like Jesus, the great Yogi-Christs of India, and the ascended masters, who exhibit this same awareness, the I AM consciousness," Frederick explained. "No one is from this planet. All are from God."

One of the more novel claims made by Frederick and John was based on Genesis 1:11 ("Let the earth bring forth grass, the herb that yields seed, and the fruit tree that yields fruit according to its kind, whose seed is in itself, on the earth"). Frederick said that a mother ship, shaped like a four-sided pyramid and measuring fifteen hundred miles square, sowed these seeds of life on Earth. It is from here that all UFOs have docked and visited our planet. "This is the New Jerusalem spoken of in John's Revelation," Frederick said.

Before the broadcast was over, Frederick and John had charted the outer realms of extraterrestrial insanity. They both claimed to have once lived in the Orion constellation where beings did not have sex but reproduced each other through "spiritual mating," by extending their gossamerlike tendrils.

For those concerned about gangs and violence and the dwindling rain forests, John had hope. "Earth is moving in its orbit closer to the galactic center, which is the seat of God," he said, "so spirituality will be on the increase."

In case Bill Clinton is reading this book, Frederick prophesied that Americans would elect a walk-in as president in the nineties!

But his parting shot was the most frightening, a warning that some walk-ins may not ask permission before taking over a human body.

After listening to such extraterrestrial nonsense I cut in on Frederick. "This is getting ridiculous," I said. "You say that all the great people of history, George Washington, Thomas Jefferson, Abraham Lincoln, Edison, even Jesus Christ were all walk-ins, bodies taken over by outer space beings. I've heard you talk for nearly an hour and have not heard a single bit of evidence for what you say. Prove it!"

Frederick exploded. "Manners are the foundation of spirituality," he said. "Don't interrupt me. I've already told you, I am one of you, but I am not one of you, and neither are you one of you. You only think you are."

"What?" I replied in shock.

"If you don't show some manners, I'll refuse to continue being on your program!"

"Hey, this is my show. You work with me, I don't work with you," I demanded.

"Look, I told you," Frederick went on. "When I took over this body I was an invisible realm of thought. I walked into this body to expose all religious frauds. I am the light and the way!"

Ironically, barely a year after the incredulous duo appeared on my talk show, the extraterrestrial hoax of Frederick von Mierers and John Andreadis blew apart. As it turns out, they were the real frauds and their scam was a marketing swindle perpetrated through their Eternal Values company.

The two sold overly priced gems, which they said were "God's thoughts condensed . . . candles in the dark . . . gateways into the dimension of ether waves to prevent you from falling into delusions." The ruse came to an end when von Mierers died, some say from AIDS caused by his gay lifestyle.[1]

While swindlers like von Mierers and Andreadis are claiming to have dropped in for an earthly visit, other people say they have been plucked off the planet for an intergalactic medical mission.

Abductions

After Dr. John Mack, a Pulitzer prize-winning Harvard Medical School faculty member, appeared on the television program *Unsolved Mysteries* to promote his book, *Abduction: Human Encounters with Aliens,* his school's dean warned him not to let his zeal for UFO research compel him to violate faculty standards. (Mack's lawyers argued the university's one-year investigation challenged his academic freedom, and the school eventually decided not to censure the professor.)

Abduction reported on his treatment of patients who say aliens abducted them for sexual experiments. Mack believes that millions have been temporarily kidnapped by space aliens. Although he admitted his stance subjected him to accusations of being kooky, Mack defended the time, energy, and money he spent on the endeavor because he has contributed to "opening people's minds to some *shift in consciousness.*"2

One alleged abductee who was counseled by Mack turned out to be a writer working undercover; she told *Time* magazine she had fooled Mack into believing that she had met President John F. Kennedy and Soviet Premier Nikita Khrushchev while aboard a UFO in 1962.3 After the deception was revealed, Mack responded by suggesting that the woman may have been abducted by aliens after all and later tried to suppress the experience.

Where does Mack think aliens come from? Not outer space. The Harvard intellectual claims they are from another dimension. That's why extraterrestrials can defy known physical laws. Like some people cited in chapter six, Dr. Mack thinks that aliens are trying to send us a message. "The fact of the matter is that we have 15 to 20 years before the psychological, moral, physical and environmental collapse of the Earth as a living entity becomes altogether a reality. This is a scientific, predictable fact if you just move the clock ahead from what's going on now."4

Those seeking an occult connection for Mack's conclusions need look no further than this statement, which is the standard New Age/metaphysical interpretation of events to come. It is also very telling that Mack has been associated with an incredible array of other occult practices. These include embracing the cult of est and experimenting with breathing techniques that simulate an LSD state, which is an old mediumistic trick. Est, the early 1980s cult headed by Werner Erhard, taught a form of radical personality transformation using severe psychological brainwashing techniques. In Zen-like fashion, Erhard claimed there is no objective reality, only direct experience (see my book *Straight Answers on the New Age*, Thomas Nelson Publishers, 1989, p. 22). Adherents of Eastern religions have for millennia practiced hyperventilation methods to induce altered states of consciousness for the purposes of deity possession.

More revealing is Mack's study of shamanism, the New Age euphemism for witchcraft. A shaman is a native or aboriginal folk healer who receives his cures and prophecies from paranormal sources (the spirit world). Obviously, Mack has no intellectual or spiritual boundaries to his occult inquiries, and therefore he has made himself vulnerable to all sorts of supernatural incursions. The same is true for many in our society who disregard the biblical injunctions against divination and enchantments (Deut. 18:9–14) and venture into the territory of demons and the devil.

ALIENS OR DEMONS?

That starry Nebraska night when I thought I saw a UFO was decades ago. Have I ever seen another one? There have been times when I've wondered if some dancing light in the distance was more than a reflection, especially when I'm driving late at night on a lonely interstate highway. I have heard unearthly sounds. I have felt strange presences. And I've wondered if what I heard or sensed might be from another reality.

Objectively speaking, there has been only one other instance when I might have seen a UFO. It happened during an intense counseling session about a dozen years ago.

For more than twenty years I have ministered to individuals who claim to be possessed by evil spirits. In some of these cases I have conducted exorcisms and encountered the supernatural realm of evil. On one such occasion, a minister and I were meeting with a woman who sought to escape a black-magic cult associated with ceremonies of satanic ritualism. In the midst of an intensive time of prayer, this woman, Denise, said she was terrorized by what she described as an alien invasion of our meeting.

Denise had been an adept of the black arts and had been assigned to call forth demons in conjuration ceremonies. Through these practices she apparently acquired the ability to peer into the spirit world. Many times during my sessions with her, she claimed to see demons and described them in vivid, exacting detail. They were no longer beautiful and enticing. Now, they revealed their true identities. They were grotesque with misshapen heads, slender bodies, elongated limbs, and clawlike digits. In fact, the pictures of these demons, which Denise drew for me, strongly resembled the sketches abductees draw of aliens.

On one occasion Denise abruptly interrupted our session and ran to the window, peering out with eyes wide and hands trembling as if she were searching for something. According to her account, some kind of spaceship had landed on the front lawn and tiny creatures, which looked demonic, disembarked. Denise frantically described the horrific features of these beings. Once off the mother craft, they each boarded a minicraft, which passed through the walls of the house. Then they hovered above us.

Denise ducked and raised her arms over her head. She ran about the room, trying to escape what she later told us were some kind of death rays, which came from the miniature UFOs. Her eyes darted back and forth and focused on what she thought were minisaucers, which were tormenting her. The horror held her captive, and she dodged first one way, then another.

The entire episode lasted nearly ten minutes, and we could not comfort her or protect her from these tormentors.

Afterward Denise was breathless and weary. She explained that the floating spacecraft had the ability to hover and dart in any direction with a dexterity that would be a challenge to a hummingbird. These diminutive saucers were trying to kill or injure her as they had done before, she told us. Then she pointed to scars on her arms, which she said were the result of previous attacks.

Her belief in the incident was so real, I was forced to consider if it might be something more than a psychotic reaction due to mental illness. However, Denise had no history of any mental aberrations or psychiatric counseling. In fact, she was a nurse who worked with the emotionally disabled.

I also asked myself if the stress of our intensive spiritual dialogue had overwhelmed her, or if for some perverse reason she had acted out this scenario. Yet Denise had never conducted herself so irrationally during any of our several previous meetings. And after this occurrence I never saw her exhibit this seemingly demented behavior again. I concluded that the attack of the miniature aliens was either an atypical mental aberration or something supernatural.

A strange story? Yes, but no more bizarre than the accounts of other UFO sightings, claimed by an array of otherwise normal people.

Other Incredible Incidents

In the summer of 1996, about the time that *Independence Day* was packing theaters nationwide, an incredible account surfaced of a close encounter similar to the incident that inspired the 1993 movie *Fire in the Sky*. That film recorded the abduction of Travis Walton twenty years ago. Travis, who lived in Snowflake, Arizona, wrote about his experience with alien creatures in a book later made into the movie. Walton was supposedly beamed up to a flying saucer by a blue light near the Arizona Mogollon Rim area. The aliens kept him captive for five days before finally dropping him off in a telephone booth in Heber, Arizona. The 1996 encounter happened just ten miles from the location of Walton's capture.

In this case, a trucker named Devin Williams was driving an eighteen-wheeler full of lettuce and strawberries from Los Angeles to Kansas on Interstate 40 in northern Arizona. Suddenly Williams went out-of-control and veered off the interstate at Winslow. He sped forty miles down a remote Arizona highway toward a Ranger Station. Then he barreled another fifteen miles on a rough Forest Service dirt road, at times menacingly circling campers or running other motorists off the road.

Williams's truck finally got stuck in the mud near the edge of the Rim. He climbed out, fell to his knees, and started talking to a tree. Then he waved a twenty dollar bill wildly in the air and threw rocks at people who tried to approach him. He pointed to a rock and said he was about to start a fire with it.

When someone asked Williams about his bizarre conduct, the trucker replied, *"They* made me do it!" Whom he was referring to, Williams wouldn't say.

What happened next was even more peculiar. The twenty-eight-year-old trucker simply disappeared, leaving behind his semi and his favorite hat—and was never seen again. Those prone to a more natural explanation say he flipped his lid and then got lost in the woods and died. But most nearby residents say, "What happened to Travis Walton was happening all over again to Devin Williams."

When Walton was asked about the Williams story, he said, "We've been having all kinds of weird things up here. Three different people told me they saw a big, orange object hit the ground right before a forest fire started."[5]

Charles Green of Tucson, Arizona, who says he has had sixteen "alien encounters" during the past fifty-five years, believes there is a striking similarity between Williams and Walton. Green, a member of the Texas-based group MUFON, asserts that such abductions are for sexual experimentation. "They take the semen from the males and the ovaries from females and mix it with alien juice to make a half-breed. What I don't understand is why they didn't bring Williams back."[6]

And other similar stories abound. A Minnesota construction worker says he definitely saw a UFO while walking to his parents' house in Kingston, Minnesota, after a day of fishing. Kim Cates, age twenty-seven, says he witnessed a large, silvery, oval object hovering in the southwest sky about one-half mile away. Cates claims the thing put him into some kind of hypnotic trance. He watched it dip and drift silently, moving west to east for about ten seconds before it vanished at a high speed.

A neighbor, who rented land on the Cates farm and had no knowledge of Kim's story, later discovered a burned circular patch of soybeans, forty feet in diameter, located on the hill where Cates had seen the flying object. After comparing stories, the neighbor and Cates concluded that the saucer had dipped near the soybeans and its radiation killed the plants.

In an age when people see the visage of Mother Teresa on cinnamon buns and the Virgin Mary on the reflective windows of a Florida office tower, can we believe *any* accounts of UFO sightings? That is open to question. But what cannot be avoided is the incredible variety of UFO accounts, which make the Ken Arnold incident (the pilot who spotted the unidentified flying objects that started the modern flying saucer craze) seem utterly conventional by comparison. And these sight-ings are worldwide.

In 1978 Italian citizens reported UFOs throughout the country for three consecutive days in mid-September. One man in Florence saw a cigar-shaped, metallic object with red lights at the front and back. A group of railway workers in Bolzano said they saw a triangular-shaped object flying low and emitting beams of light. By the third day police offices in Rome were bombarded with calls from their own patrols, as well as from numerous citizens. Most of the descriptions were of bright, triangular-shaped objects, which seemed to float over the city, beaming green-and-yellow lights. Residents of Sardinia, Sicily, and Tuscany also reported sightings.

In the late eighties, airline Captain Kenju Terauchi approached the Anchorage, Alaska, flight control tower, ask-ing if any other traffic was in the area. "Negative," was the controller's response. That answer puzzled the Japan Airlines pilot who had sat mesmerized for five minutes as two massive columns of light pierced the darkness at 35,000 feet and seemed to single out his craft for illumination. Terauchi, an experienced pilot, reported that he had never seen anything like this before on any of his international flights.

The most legendary of all UFO sighters is Eduard Meier, a thirty-eight-year-old Swiss farmer. Meier claims to have had more than a hundred contacts with UFOs and their occupants in a remote part of Canton, Zurich. He even has photos to back up his story. According to Meier, his primary contact is a female who is humanoid in appearance, except for the bluish color of her skin. The alien has told Meier that she comes from a race of beings in the star group Pleiades where their technology is thirteen thousand years ahead of ours. They're here, she says, to guide us in spiritual and technical knowledge.

Such assertions raise interesting questions about why beings out there might want to bother with us down here.

Why Are They Here?

If *they* are here, why? Is it for sexual experimentation as Charles Green suggests, or is the Swiss farmer closer to the truth when he says their intent is spiritual?

The case of Skye Ambrose of St. Charles, Missouri, points to a spiritual purpose. About six years ago Ambrose was driving down a remote, moonlit stretch of Colorado highway. Enticed by circular flashing lights in the sky, she and a friend pulled off Interstate 70, cut their headlights, and watched as ethereal black waves began to surround their car.

Then what looked like a falling star appeared. Ambrose watched the star turn into a glowing ball of white light, which stopped above a field, hovering no more than one hundred feet from the car. As the women watched in speechless amazement, two beams of light, brilliant with a spectrum of pinks, purples, and blues, shot out from the ball.

Ambrose and her friend remember hightailing it out of there and ending up in a Goodland, Kansas, motel. After Ambrose checked in, the two women went into the room and turned on the light. Ambrose's face was colorless and drawn, and her friend's complexion was deeply flushed. Their hair was plastered flat against their heads. They sensed that something wasn't right, since neither of them felt ill.

Ambrose went out and looked at the car while her friend watched from the window. Ambrose couldn't see much in the dark, but she grabbed a map out of the glove compartment.

When they looked at the map, the two women were stunned to realize it had taken three hours to drive only seventy-two miles. Somehow, somewhere, they had lost two hours.

The emotional terror Ambrose experienced following the episode led her to a psychiatric social worker who subjected her to hypnotic regressions to try to recover the missing time. Her friend did the same and both came up with identical stories, without collusion. The beams from the ball of light contained two beings, perhaps five feet tall, thin, white, and featureless except for two huge, dark eyes. They transported the women to an enormous craft in the sky, then took them to a small circular room, in which Ambrose's friend underwent surgery. The aliens implanted what looked like a small computer chip with tiny hooks deep within her friend's nose, they said.

While Ambrose watched in a semi-trance, two aliens rubbed and stroked her head to calm her. A third alien with glittering eyes held her entranced with its beguiling, mysterious orbs. Both women were then taken to the tallest of the beings who telepathically assured them that they meant no harm. The lead alien said that he and his cohorts were guardians of Earth and had been so for millions of years. They were now choosing people to do this work with them.

The effect of all this on Ambrose was so dramatic, she left her career in real estate sales and marketing and became a massage therapist. Ambrose, who says the incident has led her to spiritual growth, declares her purpose in life is to learn more about the aliens' "grand designs for evolutionary midwifery." According to Ambrose, "I know now that I chose to go through this. I'm cooperating with a universal purpose . . . to bring out evolutionary change and make sure we humans don't destroy the planet in the meantime."[7]

UFO literature is replete with tales, like Ambrose's, of

abductions for the purpose of spiritual instruction and medical examination. And if aliens implanting computer chips in someone's nose strikes you as somewhat strange, wait until you hear what aliens are supposedly doing to animals.

CHAPTER EIGHT

UFOs
and
Evil
Aliens

Willy's face was weathered from the effect of forty years of cattle ranching. The deep lines that traversed his brow told of the frigid winters in northern Alberta where thirty-below-zero temperatures were not uncommon. I met him more than ten years ago in Red Deer, a small town compared to most states or provinces, but the biggest city this side of Edmonton in this sparsely populated part of Alberta.

Willy walked up to me after I spoke one evening. He was dressed like a cowboy with a big, silver, oval buckle, a western shirt, well-worn boots, and a slightly dilapidated straw hat.

"The name's William, but you can call me Willy like everyone else," he said as he motioned for me to step aside from the crowd. He whispered, "I don't want anyone to hear what I tell you. Enough people already think I'm crazy."

At first Willy talked tentatively about who or what had mutilated his herd of cattle. I found myself questioning his sanity; maybe one too many January blizzards had altered his judgment. But after the entire story unfolded, I could not question his sincerity.

"The first livestock I found mutilated was early last fall, a prize bull. We called him Old Hannibal," Willy explained. "He was worth upwards of three thousand dollars when someone, or something, killed him. His eyes, ears, and tongue were all gone, cut out cleanly." Willy shook his head. "What really spooked me was the fact that Hannibal's blood had been drained. There wasn't a spot of blood anywhere around the carcass when I found him." Willy looked at me for my reaction.

Instead of showing any response, I apologized to the other people standing nearby, who were there to talk to me; I couldn't interrupt this man.

"I heard that you know a lot about this occult stuff, so I came to tell you about what happened to me. Any idea who or what did it?" Willy asked.

"Are there any mountain lions in this part of the country?"

"Nope," Willy replied. "It's a good two hundred miles to Jasper from where I live, and no one has seen a cougar anywhere near these parts for at least thirty years."

"How about a pack of coyotes?"

"Plenty of them around, but if you'd seen the condition Hannibal was in, you'd know it wasn't coyotes. Even the Royal Canadian Mounted Police officer who came to check it out said that the cuts were too sharp to be a predator. Plus, the ground is muddy that time of year, and there were no tracks anywhere. In fact, I found Hannibal at the top of a ridge, and there weren't any hoof marks near his body. I don't know how he got up there."

Willy motioned for me to lean down lower. His voice was barely audible. "What frightened me was the heifer I found about a month after Hannibal was killed," he went on. "She weighed about five hundred pounds and was one of the finest Herefords I've ever seen. Her sex organs had been cut off and her rectum removed. Whoever did it made a perfectly round incision. Mr. Larson, no animal could do that. They'd rip at the flesh. Anyway, no coyote or whatever would go just for the private parts and leave the rest of the flesh behind. No way!"

Occult Mutilations?

Though Willy's story was the initial first-person account I heard about animal mutilations, I had read similar anecdotes in newspapers. In the 1970s about ten thousand cattle were found dead, their body parts and vital organs precisely removed. More than three dozen states in the U.S.A. had reports, as well as several Canadian provinces and areas as far away as Puerto Rico, South America, Panama, and Europe. Speculative theories ranged from satanic sacrifices to suspicions that the federal government was using livestock for germ-warfare tests or some sort of environmental experimentation.

In Iowa, where a large number of cattle were killed, the Department of Criminal Investigations (DCI) targeted several devil-worshiping cults. Investigators discovered abandoned Iowa farmhouses with satanic writings on the walls and floors, indicating ceremonies had been held there. When DCI officials went to the Des Moines Public Library to consult books on satanism, every volume on the subject was gone. Library officials refused to turn over their circulation records and sought an injunction against the investigators to keep the files private,

As was promised – the keys to Heaven's Gate are here again as Ti and Do (The UFO Two) as they were in Jesus and His Father 2000 yrs. ago...

The logo the Heaven's Gate cult used on its Website. The cult believed there was an extraterrestrial world of advanced aliens awaiting followers, and the only way to get there was through Heaven's Gate.

This is a representation of one of the Kingdom of Heaven aliens, whom Heaven's Gate cult members believed would come and beam them aboard a UFO hiding in the tail of the Hale-Bopp comet.

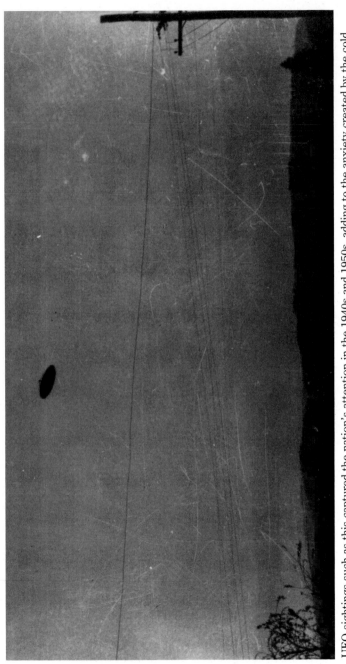

UFO sightings such as this captured the nation's attention in the 1940s and 1950s, adding to the anxiety created by the cold war, the space race with the Soviet Union, and the radio drama "War of the Worlds." *Photo by UPI/Corbis-Bettmann*

A New Mexico State University student took this photograph of an unidentified flying object while shooting geological structures. New Mexico has been the site of many UFO encounters, including the famous Roswell incident in which authorities recovered four supposed alien bodies. *Photo by UPI/Corbis-Bettmann*

Scientists from NASA's Johnson Space Center in Houston said in August 1996 that they had discovered evidence of "life," carbonate mineral globules similar to fossilized bacteria, in this meteorite from Mars. *Photo by AP/Wide World Photos*

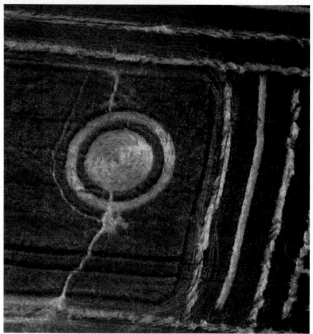

Residents of Butte, Nebraska, found a thirty-five-foot crop circle in a barley field in July 1996. Believed to be created by alien spacecraft, most crop circles show no signs of tracks or other human intervention. In this case, the tracks leading to the crop circle were made by hundreds of visitors to the site after the discovery. *Photo by AP/Wide World Photos*

A Hope, Arkansas, farmer found four of his pregnant heifers laying dead in a straight line on his land on March 10, 1989. Three had rectum tissue excised in clean, bloodless ovals. One had an eye removed, and another had an 18-inch by 22-inch section of its belly removed. *Photo by Juanita Stripling, Little River (Ark.) News*

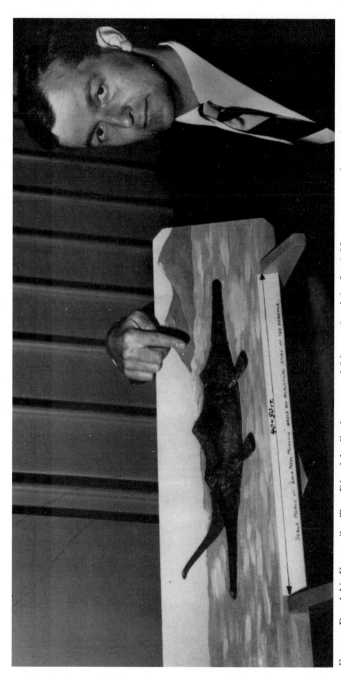

Former Royal Air Force pilot Tom Dinsdale displays a model he made of the Loch Ness monster after seeing the legendary creature in 1960. He said he even captured the creature on film as it swam and dived in the Scottish lake.

Photo by UPI/Corbis-Bettmann

Doctors from the supersecret Majestic 12 government agency examine an alien on the NBC television series "Dark Skies." A real MJ-12 group was supposedly started in 1947 after authorities discovered "four small human-like beings" in a crash site in Roswell, New Mexico. © *Photo by Columbia Pictures Television*

Uriel, also known as Ruth Norman, stands by her Space Cadillac on a landing strip constructed for flying saucers. Uriel, the founder of the Unarius Foundation who died in 1993, said in her will that she would pick up the car when she returns to Earth with her spacefleet in 2001.

Photo © 1997 by Michael Grecco / Sygma

with the support of the Iowa Civil Liberties Union. The Iowa Witches Association confronted the DCI; they insisted that their membership consisted of only good witches who would never intentionally harm animals.

A sociologist in Iowa's neighbor to the northwest, at the University of South Dakota, dismissed any talk of a satanic cabal. Professor James Stewart declared that the mutilations were an example of "mass mild hysteria." He postulated that the killings were the work of predators who devoured only the softest parts of the carcasses. The sharp side teeth of the marauding animals accounted for the well-defined cuts, he argued.[1]

Yet investigators in Alberta, Canada, determined that human beings were responsible because of the skillful nature of the incisions. While it is true that some satanic cults practice animal sacrifices, the Canadian authorities decided that the mutilations were not done in the typical manner of most devil-worshiping cults. The Canadians finally decided on this theory: The first few mutilations were of human origin, possibly satanic cult splinter groups, but the mass of mutilations were the work of copycats, duplicating methods they had read about in media reports.

OTHER EXPLANATIONS

In Colorado, the state that has experienced the most cattle mutilations, the deputy chief of the Colorado Bureau of Investigation looked into two hundred dead-livestock cases. He claimed that only ten were actually mutilated, and in each of those ten cases the animal had died from natural causes before it was mutilated. The deputy finally gave up on the investigation. Human beings were being shot at and murdered every day, and he reasoned that spending his time on crimes against people was a more productive use of law enforcement resources.

The talk among some ranchers turned to speculation that sexual deviates were getting their kicks by detaching sexual organs. Others thought that the animals might have been caught in the crossfire of some weird form of guerrilla warfare. A Kansas State University veterinarian, who autopsied several of the cattle victims, said a disease called blackleg killed most of them. (Blackleg attacks the muscles and forms a toxic gas that enters the bloodstream.) After they were dead, the coyotes cleaned up, making it look macabre.

Nebraska got into the act when a Custer County sheriff investigated the killing of a cow, which he described as being slaughtered under "really kind of weird" circumstances.[2] The cow's blood was gone, and there was no wound, other than a slit through the hide on the abdomen. The udder and two teats were cut off. No tracks were near the body, and, when an autopsy was performed, the only blood discovered in the animal was a clot in one artery.

In New Mexico, the conclusion was different. Gabe Valdez, a northern New Mexico patrolman, suggested that something very sophisticated was behind it all. He checked out ninety cases and found many instances where the blood had been drained from the animals. There were needle marks in the jugular vein, bruises on the legs, and metal elements in the liver. More mysteriously, Valdez encountered tales of mysterious silent helicopters and circular marks on the ground.

"It's either UFOs or the government," he concluded. "Every time we have a mutilation you hear about mystery aircraft that fly 3,000 miles an hour."[3]

The UFO-Mutilation Connection

Disease? Predators? Individual weirdos? Satanic cults? UFOs?

The UFO explanation continues to take precedence over

the idea that cults are involved. Investigators say that when groups are responsible for any crime, sooner or later a member comes forward and supplies information. In the nearly three decades that animal mutilations have been publicly reported, not one cultist has ever admitted to being involved.

When thirteen reports of dead and mutilated cattle turned up in Elbert County, Colorado, in a period of less than three months, the Colorado Bureau of Investigation examined the carcasses. They determined that a sharp knife had made the original cuts to remove the scrotums, testicles, and rectums. In every case no human or vehicle tracks were seen around the animal remains. In one case the local sheriff spent three hours circling the area in widening arcs to search for any evidence but found nothing.

Ranchers whose livestock were mutilated almost universally spoke of seeing some sort of aircraft. Some suggested that a helicopter, or some kind of hovering craft, picked up the animals, transported them to another location for mutilation, and then returned them by dropping them from the air, hence the lack of tracks around the bodies.

LASER SURGERY?

The unprovable idea of alien aircraft led to the speculation that people with lasers might have been responsible for the clean cuts on the animals. This also helped to explain why no blood was found in such cases, since lasers would have sealed off the blood vessels as they penetrated the tissue. Yet if the cuts were made at the location, the vehicle to transport the laser would have left a trail since the kind of laser necessary to make the proper incision would have weighed hundreds of pounds, would have required an experienced medical technician on the scene, and would have been powered by AC current.

That was not possible in the remote ranchland setting. But if the animal were airlifted to the laser location, maybe . . .

As people reported more and more mutilations, even stranger facts emerged. For example, in Cripple Creek, Colorado, a rancher fed his horse one evening and then found him lying dead in the snow twelve hours later. The horse had a twelve-inch-wide by twelve-inch-deep, cone-shaped hole in the rectum. One eye had turned a silver color. There were no predator tracks or footprints in the snow around the mutilated horse and no signs of blood or a struggle.

MUTILATIONS ACCORDING TO HYPNOSIS

In the early eighties, an unusual report of cattle mutilations specifically linked them to UFOs. Professor Leo Sprinkle, formerly of the University of Wyoming, one of the world's leading authorities on alleged UFO abductions, encountered the strange case, which was revealed on a Denver CBS-affiliate television station. Titled *A Strange Harvest,* the documentary, produced by Linda Moulton Howe, originally aired on April 1, 1983.

When subjected to memory recall induced by hypnosis, a woman named Pat McGuire reported a bizarre encounter. With her brother, Mark, she found a dead cow on their ranch. The nose was cut off, the tongue removed, and the sex organs gone. Suddenly they looked up in the sky and saw what looked like a bright star headed their way. Then its color changed from pure white to orange. Pat and Mark watched the UFO pick up the cow and disappear with it. The cow was never seen again.

In another instance, Professor Sprinkle hypnotized a woman who described a UFO sucking a calf up into its spaceship chamber. She watched as the aliens dissected the animal while alive and then probed its flesh with needles connected to a tube.

How was she able to see what was going on in the spacecraft while she was still on the ground? The woman explained it was like an out-of-body experience, being in two places at the same time. She reluctantly told her story because she said the beings who examined the calf told her telepathically that her seeing the experiment was an accident.

The most interesting part of this hypnotherapeutic account was the woman's description of the two beings. They were short in stature with long claws on their fingers and large, unblinking eyes that looked like those of a "snake." When asked if she were frightened, the woman replied that she sensed all this was being done for the betterment of mankind, that these beings were "watching out for us."[4]

Further Evidence for an Alien Explanation

The UFO theory has been further buttressed by the finding of tripod-like marks in the ground near many of the cattle mutilation sites. In some cases the tripod marks were pressed at least eight to ten inches in the ground. Farmers and ranchers observed that it would take a post-hole digger or a shovel to make such a deep depression. Were these marks the indications of a UFO landing site? Or were they the stabilization points for some kind of crane to lift the cattle, a transporter? Either explanation is possible.

In Colorado one county undersheriff reported that while patrolling one night he saw strange lights near a cattle mutilation scene. An orange ball came up from the ground and traveled toward him. As it approached the car, the light made an immediate ninety-degree turn. The undersheriff declared he could see lights in the cockpit, one red, one white, and one green or blue. Then the lights vanished and whatever had approached him was gone.

ALIEN HELICOPTERS?

Observers have also frequently sighted helicopters near mutilation scenes. In fact, in a disturbing number of mutilations, people have reported a helicopter-like craft prior to or immediately after discovering the dead animal. What each sighting apparently has in common is that the helicopters had no identifying marks. According to all reports, the copters were silent.

The *Strange Harvest* documentary showed an interview with a battalion helicopter pilot who stated, "If I had to choose between aliens coming down and doing these things to the animals and lifting [them] as compared to a helicopter of our size . . . doing these things, I would probably be more apt to choose the alien aspect . . . than the military [copter] or any type of small helicopter."[5]

A final theory about cattle mutilations involves vampire-like creatures called goatsuckers.

GOATSUCKERS

They're known as *chupacabras* in Spanish, *goatsuckers* in English. The name came from Mexican farmers plagued by unidentified creatures that kill livestock and pets by sucking their blood. To skeptics, goatsuckers are the Mexican equivalent of the cattle mutilation myth, a folklore legend hyperbolically describing the death of animals—especially goats—caused naturally by wolves, dogs, coyotes, pumas, or giant bats (depending on the geographic region).

Goatsucker sightings started in Puerto Rico and spread to

the U.S. mainland via the Hispanic community in Florida. There the victims were ducks, chickens, and domestic animals. Once the phenomenon reached Mexico, full-blown hysteria ensued, especially after some humans claimed they had been attacked. The victims said they saw a clawed creature with black membranous wings come down from the night sky and descend upon them. Fear reached such proportions in Mexico City, the civil defense forces were called to homes in neighborhoods where the vampire-creature was said to have appeared.

Eventually a *chupacabra* symposium was called at a Mexico City University. Goatsucker songs became popular and a TV wrestler took the goatsucker name. All along, comparisons were made with the North American preoccupation with UFOs. Other speculation suggested that the goatsucker stories were revamped vampire stories.

Undeterred by the logic of detractors, farmers who believe in goatsuckers say that a vampire-like creature is on the loose ravaging their herds. Their proof is the two tooth marks that measure approximately a third of an inch each, found in the neck area of their dead livestock. Some describe three puncture wounds, but whatever the number, they are all concentrated in the neck area.

Mexican governmental authorities do not subscribe to the *chupacabra* theory and instead attribute the phenomenon to hysteria. Officials say that when veterinarians do autopsies on dead animals, they discover a variety of causes of death, none of which supports the theory.

Has anyone seen a goatsucker? Thousands say yes, and have come forward with amazingly similar descriptions. Some say the creature jumped like a kangaroo and smelled like sulphur. Others say it was more like a monkey or a tiger. But in general it is usually depicted as half animal, half human with huge, bulging red eyes and short arms. Its fingers have sharp claws and there are spikes down the back of the spine. The goatsucker can also fly. As proof of a paranormal predator, some say they have found footprints that resemble those of a large ape.

Theories about the origin of *chupacabras* vary from location to location. In Puerto Rico, some attribute the bloodsucking deaths to an unidentified animal, like a rhesus monkey, erroneously let loose on the island. But equally fervent Puerto Ricans offer a more exotic explanation. They say that aliens are drawn to the island by the Arecibo Observatory, the world's largest radio-radar telescope, the one used in SETI research, mentioned in chapter six.

In defense of those who claim they have seen a *chupacabra,* the sighters are mostly rural people who have spent a lifetime around livestock and would presumably know the signs of a typical predator that would attack their herds. In fact, some who say they have seen the creature were so traumatized by the experience they were taken to hospitals. Now they are demanding action from governmental officials because of the threat *chupacabras* pose to their economic livelihood.

Why Mutilate Animals?

Let's suppose these bizarre mutilations *are* connected to UFOs in some way. The first question ought to be: Why would UFOs target animals for eccentric experiments?

Those who argue against a UFO explanation reason that no intelligent extraterrestrial would intentionally leave a mass of carcasses all over the planet. If ETs were performing experiments on earth life-forms, they would surely have hidden the remains or mutilated them less precisely to make it appear that predators were responsible.

UFO enthusiasts counter that the carcasses are deliberately left with evidence of systematic mutilation. What better way to stimulate our curiosity about what is happening and who is doing it? Such terror by design would disarm investigators, and would also incite earthlings to look for paranormal explanations.

Unexplained animal mutilations would facilitate a conditioning process for earth beings to accept the presence of alien visitors. From that point onward it would only be a matter of time until aliens would inaugurate actual ET-to-human contact.

Or perhaps these beings want random samples of the flesh of large animals. The excised organs might be the repository of certain chemicals, or the organs might reveal radiation levels.

One psychic has suggested that aliens, ancient beings in surveillance of this planet, are collecting serum to return to mankind during a time of need. It should be no surprise to readers of this book that some mutilations occurred near sites of crop circles.

The mania surrounding extraterrestrials and other unexplained creatures seems to stem from a modern mistrust of the ability of science to solve mankind's problems, and evolution's inability to explain unusual creature sightings. More and more, people forego a religious view of reality; but at the same time they distrust the premise that science has all the answers. As a result, they fall victim to occult and paranormal speculation.

This mind-set is accentuated by the ambivalence of people to trust either in the natural world of observation or the supernatural world of angels and demons. In this atmosphere of uncertainty, belief in a God who cannot be seen must take a back seat to the apparent "evidence" of unidentified creatures. After all, at least these beings make their presence known, albeit in strange ways.

The media has rushed into this spiritual vacuum to exploit all sorts of tales about bloodsucking evil aliens, constantly making them bigger and more fearsome than their network competitors. Unfortunately, the information dispensed in movies and on television is too often slanted toward pop hysteria and misinformation.

In a way, speculation about cattle mutilations and goatsuckers has become a quasi religion. Throughout recorded history there has been a theological bond between life and blood. The ancient Hebrew Scriptures address this linkage: "Only be sure that you do not eat the blood, for the blood is the life . . ." (Deut. 12:23). It should not surprise us that various evil aliens would seek the blood of humans and animals as a means of spiritual deception. And it should come as no shock that humanity, which has largely rejected the God of the Bible, would look to exotic, bloodthirsty explanations for the origin and purpose of life on Earth.

Are human beings the next victims? Will aliens kidnap humans, lift them in the air to waiting spaceships, remove their vital organs, then drop them again to Earth? Could humans become the target of aliens who want to harvest DNA to create biological clones through some superior technology? It has not happened yet, or at least there have been no credible published reports, only the questionable abductee hypnosis accounts. (Rumors persist that human mutilations have occurred, but criminal investigators who fear public hysteria have explained them away.)

An intriguing question is why the sightings have fallen off in recent years. Perhaps the press has grown tired of mutilation stories and the lack of an answer has created a general public skepticism or denial. Or maybe whoever is responsible for the phenomenon has already gathered enough information so that their aerial laboratories need no additional specimens.

Another theory suggests that certain superior alien civilizations have entered into a secret treaty with the world's governments to garner animals and humans as needed for experimentation. They are permitted to carry on this activity uncontested in exchange for their promise not to launch a military attack against Earth. Indeed, purported secret documents distributed among UFO enthusiasts suggest that various government agencies are aware of ETs, which periodically visit Earth to benevolently manipulate the DNA of humans.

I believe the real answer is twofold. First, those who have escaped certain satanic cults have confirmed to me that the harvesting of animal sexual organs serves an important ritualistic purpose. In addition, some satanic cults perform baptismal ceremonies by immersing the initiates in blood. This requires a large amount of blood, so they drain the blood of big mammals.

Second, I am convinced that some percentage of mutilations, which cannot be explained away naturally, are indeed the acts of evil aliens, and the agenda of these spirit beings is the spiritual terrorization of the population. As I will now show, these evil spirits hide their agenda by taking on many different manifestations.

CHAPTER NINE

The Alien Index

Their eyes resembled soft-boiled eggs with irises stuck to them. Their oversized humanoid skulls bulged with an externalized excess of gray matter. Their brain tissue was exposed in convoluted ridges on the outside of their heads. Devoid of lips, their bared teeth chattered like windup toys found in novelty stores. The aliens of Tim Burton's *Mars Attacks!* were more goofball than gruesome.

Hoping to cash in on the *Independence Day* craze, *Mars Attacks!*, released in December 1996, featured a big-name cast, including Jack Nicholson, Glenn Close, Pierce Brosnan, Sarah Jessica Parker, Martin Short, and Michael J. Fox. These Hollywood luminaries were pitted against absurdly evil Martians who bumped them off one by one while also zapping Washington, Vegas, Big Ben, the Eiffel Tower, and Easter Island. What this sci-fi schlock lacked in logic, it made up for in oddball eccentricities.

It is an anomaly that in today's alien-crazed movie market anyone would spend $70 million making such a ridiculous film. How close did this movie come to depicting real aliens?

Portrait of an Alien

Contactees say that no two aliens look alike. But there are enough similarities to come up with a composite portrait.

The aliens involved in a close encounter have abnormally huge heads and enormous eyes that are set wide apart and seem to bulge. The mouth and nose are barely noticeable; at most, the mouth is a horizontal slit. They may have large, pointed ears.

A few witnesses say they have seen aliens with short wings and tails. Their arms are long with large hands and long nails or claws. They generally have a humanoid resemblance but with very thin limbs. In reference to the most-quoted misperception, they seldom have green skin. Most are no more than three or four feet tall.

Aliens are usually silent, communicating by gestures or mental telepathy. Those that do emit sounds grunt like pigs or speak in guttural, chattery tones as if vocalizing from a pipe. Some make shrill sounds similar to a gargle. A few have musical dialects with a childlike quality.

Who really knows what is true? Let's look at the theories that are most fashionable today.

THREE TYPES OF ALIENS

Sifting through the many volumes of UFO reports shows that aliens spotted in close encounters are usually classified as one of three types: (1) humanoid (usually referred to as the Nordics, the Grays, or the Men in Black); (2) nonhumanoid (generally known as reptilians); or (3) hybrids (which are aliens crossbred with humans). Distinctives regarding sex are harder to come by. Though most have appeared as males, a few humanoid aliens looked like spacewomen.

HUMANOID ALIENS

Descriptions of humanoid aliens have changed vastly over the last five decades. When first sighted, they appeared slim and handsome, with long blond hair. These so-called blond Venusians appeared in the California desert and as far away as South America. The Venusians apparently had cosmic brothers, more Nordic-looking creatures, who were also pale-skinned and blue-eyed. The original sighting of Nordics caused some ufologists to speculate that these creatures were descended from German rocket scientists who made contact with extraterrestrials. The Venusians supposedly had a secret base for their craft in the Antarctic.

In the middle decades of this century, the humanoid aliens who contacted earthlings sometimes did so for sex. In 1957 a much-publicized incident involved a Brazilian farmer who claimed he was taken aboard a UFO by small beings who undressed him and left him alone in a chamber. Then a tall, naked woman, with elongated eyes and straight white hair, entered the room. After an act of sexual intercourse, the Brazilian said the alien pointed to her abdomen, apparently signaling that he had been abducted to breed a humanoid hybrid.

The Grays are the most commonly reported humanoid aliens of today. They have protracted oval eyes, long thin arms and legs, and slits for noses and mouths. The name *Gray* comes from the color of their skin. Whitley Strieber's books (which I'll discuss in chapter ten) have helped popularize the image of Grays, and this is the most prevalent portrait that comes to mind when people think about aliens. Grays are also described as having a large, wide mouth without teeth. Their noses are grossly oversized as if cartoon-like.

The Men in Black (referred to in UFO parlance as MIBs) are a popular folklore caricature of these humanoid aliens. The MIBs consist of groups of men (usually three) wearing sunglasses, dark hats, and black clothing. They are sometimes seen driving old black Cadillacs and apparently are on a mission to harass those who claim to have seen flying saucers and threaten them into silence. They also show up at the homes of UFO abductees, ordering them to keep quiet. A 1997 sci-fi adventure action comedy, entitled *Men in Black*, featured Will Smith and Tommy Lee Jones in a funny take-off of *Independence Day*.

NONHUMANOID ALIENS

The nonhumanoid aliens described by some UFO abductees share enough characteristics with *Homo sapiens* to avoid being classified as animals. Some of these beings are associated with the legendary tales of creatures like Bigfoot and the Abominable Snowman or with stories of little hairy dwarfs. Dwarf aliens fall into the goblin or fairy category. They usually have huge ears and long, dangling arms. About two to three feet in stature, they resemble trolls.

But the scariest of these not-quite-humanoid aliens are the reptilians. The American Museum of Natural History in New York City once put on an exhibit of models and paintings of dinosaurs. The display included a fiberglass, life-sized model of a reptilian-humanoid being, which showed what intelligent life might be like if it had descended from reptiles rather than apelike primates. The replica, about five feet tall, with claws and catlike eyes, looks much like the UFO occupants described by abductees. Some ufologists have wondered if a prehistoric creature somehow survived undetected. Indeed, tales of reptilian-humanoid sightings have surfaced at various times throughout history in many parts of the globe.

The reptilian aliens connected to UFOs originated in the occult legend of a serpent super-race who created humankind, imparted forbidden knowledge, interbred with us, and watched over our development. Today they are said to exercise mind control of human captives and perform medical procedures on them and other Earth creatures as they see fit.

These "watchers" or "custodians" are said to be preparing humanity for coming global changes. Tabloid-style magazines of questionable journalistic integrity, such as *Fate*, have published extensive analyses of how reptilians serve as well-meaning guardians of humankind. Apparently, their custodianship is at times compassionate, but at other times it is fearsome.[1]

Supporters of this hypothesis about reptilian aliens point to the widespread legends of serpent-gods feared and worshiped from China to Central America. In the ancient religions of these regions, the serpent represented divine heritage and royalty. To UFO enthusiasts, the reptilians have the ability to mesmerize their captives with one look from their golden, vertically slit pupils.

The faces of reptilians are said to be a cross between a human and a snake. With lizard-like scales and clawlike four-fingered hands, they stand about seven feet tall. The most frightening legends surrounding them are the stories of their sexual conquests of earthlings.

Reptilian-alien advocates say that proof of their theory is found in the ancient writings of Mesopotamia. They claim that antediluvian clay tablets, when translated, tell about a Sumerian god called An, leader of an extraterrestrial race called the Anunaki. One of An's sons, Enki, supposedly was the serpent of Eden who gave humanity the fruit of the tree of knowledge. Later, Enki genetically altered the indigenous species of Earth, creating hybrid beings. Eventually, Enki and his ilk accelerated the evolution of man, an intervention that explains the so-called missing link in the hominid line.

Note how the UFO theory of reptilian aliens explains away the significance of Holy Scripture. This hypothesis, partially based on occult Jewish texts, suggests that the Bible's account of the Garden of Eden is backward. Yes, a reptile tempted humanity with the knowledge of good and evil, but this being was no loathsome serpent. He stood upright like a tall man, possessed a superior intellect, and was king over all the animals.

This serpent became envious of the conjugal rights of the man and the woman, and thus devised a way to get them to disobey their reptilian creator. Adam and Eve's fall from grace was a retrogression from their created reptilian condition to a less desirable, spiritually limited mammalian nature. Ever since, other reptilian guardians of humanity have been coaxing us back to our pre-Edenic reptilian glory. This, then, is the purpose for reptilian-alien visitations.

To make matters more confusing, some speculate that alien-human crossbreeding has produced considerable genetic diversity.

HYBRIDS OR CROSSBRED ALIENS

Exactly how the different types of aliens associate with each other is not known, but UFO lore assumes that some interaction, perhaps cohabitation, has occurred. Some abductees claim they were shown breeding rooms, where hybrid fetuses were grown in test tubes, like some surreal alien hydroponic garden. Certain abductees go even further.

They say they saw nurseries full of crossbred infants of varying ages who were being prepared for some bizarre fate.

Where do these aliens and their UFOs come from?

WHERE DO ALIENS COME FROM?

Speculation about the origin of UFOs and their occupants has changed with each age. While the consensus is that these beings are otherworldly in origin, *which* world is open to debate. Occultists, anxious for a validation of the lost civilization of Atlantis, suppose that aliens come from an undersea society as yet undiscovered by oceanographic exploration. The hollow-earth advocates say flying saucers come from a cavity inside Earth's sphere, a suggestion roundly denounced by geophysicists.

A more fanciful idea is that UFOs are piloted by creatures, living right next to us, in our atmosphere, who are capable of hiding in thin air—or hyperspace, to put it in today's parlance. The most metaphysically inclined suggest that aliens come from a dimension of reality concurrent with ours but a psychic step beyond our awareness. Wherever they come from, it is clear they are not of our race and are not confined by our human limitations.

Monsters in Our Midst

Many UFO seekers ignore biblical guidelines and venture into the unknown without a spiritual compass. They desperately search for something out there to prove we are not alone in the universe. This quest can take the form of an interest in unidentified creatures from outer space or in unidentified beings here on this planet. These latter creatures do more than go bump in the night. Their existence is found in the lore of many cultures. The suspicion that "things" remain unde-tected in the water, hidden in the forests, and lurking in remote locations has fascinated the curious for centuries.

There is even a name for it. The study of these unknown creatures is called cryptozoology. (The word was coined by Dr. Bernard Heuvelmans, who has interested himself in the mysterious aspects of the animal kingdom.) These beasts are said to be lurking all over the planet. They may be known as Bigfoot or Sasquatch, Yeti or the Abominable Snowman, and Almas or Wildmen. For centuries these secret monsters of the sea, lakes, and land have been the source of intense interest.

Even on today's crowded globe, there are abundant natural hiding places. The oceans are wide and deep, with some trenches plunging 36,000 feet! Though not as immense as they once were, equatorial rain forests still abound. Huge por-tions of the Himalayas and the polar caps remain unexplored. Like the astronomer who calculates that among the billions of galaxies the statistical odds are that other life exists, some anthropologists argue that there are enough uncharted areas of the Earth to conceal any number of unexposed oddities.

Let's look at the kinds of unidentified creatures on Earth, which are celebrated in legend and lore.

BIGFOOT

Its mysterious traits include a forty-inch stride, broad shoulders, and large pendulous breasts on females. Other fea-tures? Reddish-black hair and a sloping forehead that peaks at a high point near the back of the head, like the massive skull of a gorilla. Its thick arms swing in accompaniment to its lop-ing gait. Because of its fourteen-inch-long footprints it is known as Bigfoot.

She, and he, have been caught on film, spotted lurking in forests, and photographed in grainy profile. To some it's a hoax, but to others, this monster, also known in the Pacific Northwest as Sasquatch, is a giant bogeyman, immensely strong and serenely secretive.

Throughout history people have spotted similar hairy bipeds. Legend suggests they are a kind of missing link, representing a niche somewhere between *Homo sapiens* and animals. These creatures lurk on the outer fringes of civilizations, making occasional appearances to whet the appetite of those who say man's nearest ancestor is closer than we think.

Even though civilization has deforested much of the planet and pushed back the boundaries of most wildlife, these monsters won't disappear.

To most scientists these are all myths and fairy tales. They concede that every year a few new spiders, snakes, and birds turn up in remote tropical forests or deserts, but nothing so dramatic as an eight-foot-tall, bearded, menacing being. The world is too well traveled for anything the size of Bigfoot to show up suddenly in the bush. Since scientists have the technology to discover the most minute details of the plant and animal kingdoms, how could these creatures escape detection and all their remains vanish?

And there is no such thing as a true wilderness, scientists say. Orbiting satellite cameras have now photographed virtually every square inch of Earth's surface. No creatures. No way. Case closed.

In spite of every attempt at demystification by the critics, however, the myth of Bigfoot still won't go away, especially in his incarnation as the legendary Abominable Snowman.

YETI, THE ABOMINABLE SNOWMAN
The Himalayan regions of India, Nepal, and Tibet abound with stories of several such mysterious creatures inhabiting the highlands. Nepalese Sherpas insist they have repeatedly

seen his tracks in the land of perpetual snow, far above the heights where humans live.

Westerners first learned about Yeti at the turn of the century when British explorer L. A. Waddell reported seeing large footprints in the snow of the high peaks near Sikkim. The tale was largely ignored until 1921 when an expedition climbed the north face of Mount Everest. At the 17,000-foot level the adventurers saw dark figures moving on a snowfield. When they reached the spot, the creatures had disappeared, leaving behind humanlike footprints in the snow. The group's leader recounted the incident to journalists in India and called the elusive creature by its Nepalese designation. That word got lost in the transmission to the western world and was phonetically translated as *Abominable Snowman.*

Immediately, reported sightings of huge footprints and large creatures poured in from around the world. Mountain climbers found tracks in the high mountain realms of southern Asia. The sightings multiplied so fast that some concluded there must be several kinds of Snowmen.

During the following decades, various expeditions set out to capture or photograph Yeti. Even the famous Sir Edmund Hillary, the first man to scale Mt. Everest, the world's tallest mountain, headed up a 1960 effort. Hillary examined footprints, furs, and scalps, but concluded there was no scientific basis for the legend of the Abominable Snowman. In Hillary's view, it all amounted to nothing more than a "fascinating fairy tale, born of the rare and frightening view of strange animals, molded by superstition and enthusiastically nurtured by Western expeditions."[2]

Still, Sherpas believed that the famous Khumjung Yeti scalp, hundreds of years old, was all the evidence they needed. The scalp, conical in shape, was about eight inches high and had a base circumference of twenty-six inches. When it was brought to the West, scientists claimed it was the scalp of a mountain goat. Yet such debunking has not deterred the claims of those living near the Himalayas. At one point the Bhutan government issued commemorative stamps portraying various versions of the Snowman, designated as their national animal.

Perhaps the biggest impediment to further research is the mythic way Sherpas describe Yeti's appearance on Earth. Supposedly, a monkey king was converted to Buddhism and lived as a hermit in the mountains. An ogress fell in love with him, and he abandoned his solitary life to marry her. The children she bore him were covered in hair and had tails. They were the first Yeti. Such superstition calls into question many Sherpa sightings, because they could be the result of visionary fantasies caused by mythic speculation. However, it might be argued that the Yeti came first and apocryphal stories, such as the monkey king, followed later.

The most reasonable assumption, according to scientists, is that if Yeti exists he may be a descendant of the giant prehistoric ape *Gigantopithecus*, which supposedly roamed southern Asia 500,000 years ago. At that time the Himalayas were believed to be rising thousands of feet and the Yeti may have become isolated in the tallest peaks on Earth.

ALMAS AND WILDMEN

Other legends of Yeti-like creatures are common in the regions of Mongolia. There they are called Almas, or Wildmen. They are considered a race of lesser humans but are not considered harmful. Russian and Mongolian scholars who have researched the Almas report characteristics similar to those of the Abominable Snowman, except that the Mongolian monsters are nocturnal.

The most striking aspect of these creatures are the tales of human cohabitation. In one case humans are said to have impregnated a captive Alma several times, and she later bore several offspring. The half-breed babies were supposed to be mostly like humans, but were unruly and extremely strong. These stories led some researchers to conclude that the Almas were remnant Neanderthals, a human subspecies biologically similar to man.

A breed of hairy hominoid is also said to roam the People's Republic of China. There the creature is called Wildman. Sightings have been reported for centuries. The western world first became aware of Wildman during the fifties. Most reported cases turned out to be monkeys called gibbons; however, some Wildmen were said to be seven feet tall, too large for a gibbon. Though no one ever captured a Wildman specimen, some people found hair samples that seemed to be from no known animal. Many Chinese scientists are convinced that a large, nocturnal, omnivorous primate roams the thickets of vast forests, which have changed little over the millennia and present a stable environment to support the Wildman's habitat.

SASQUATCH

If historians are correct that the first humans reached the North American continent by a land bridge from Asia, who can argue against the possibility that Almas and Wildmen came with them? Accounts of hairy giants have persisted among some American Indians of the Pacific Northwest. The name *Sasquatch,* meaning "wild man of the woods," comes from the Salish Indian tribe of British Columbia. In the early nineteenth century Sasquatch was supposedly seen in the region of Morris Mountain, about sixty or so miles inland from Vancouver. For the next one hundred years there were sporadic reports of sightings, but most critics relegated it all to hoaxes, delusions, or superstitious Indian legends.

But as reports of Yeti captivated newspaper readers in the early 1950s, reports of Sasquatch once again turned up. Several researchers dedicated their lives to tailing the hairy creature. John Green, a British Columbia newsman, was the most ardent of all. Another avid investigator, Rene Dahinden, spent thirty years in pursuit of the monster. Green and Dahinden joined forces and eventually connected with a retired lumberman, Albert Ostman, who told them the fantastic tale of being abducted by an entire family of Sasquatches.

Ostman described his captors as being eight feet tall with six-inch-long hair on their bodies. They treated him gently but would not allow him to leave. Ostman remained sequestered for six days before escaping. When he returned to civilization, the lumberman kept quiet about the incident for fear he would be considered insane. In fact, he said nothing for thirty-three years—until he meet Green and Dahinden. Then Ostman unfolded his mysterious tale and the two published it across Canada.

The most notable appearance of Sasquatch was in a roll of twenty feet of film, taken in October 1967 near Bluff Creek, California. One-time rodeo worker, Roger Patterson, shot the film, he said, on the outskirts of a dense forest. The 16mm movie is jumpy because Patterson was on the run. The creature looked to be about seven feet high and weighed nearly four hundred pounds. Skeptics noted that the animal had a center of gravity much like a modern man and ambled with a self-conscious walk, like that of a bad actor.

Believers say the reason Sasquatch has never been found is because of the inhospitable terrain of his mountain home, impassable gorges and ravines, which have frustrated searchers. Some caves near Morris Mountain showed signs of past habitation, though whether by long-dead Indians or hairy hominids, no one can say.

Meanwhile, people sighted shaggy giants across the United States—in Ohio, Michigan, and as far east as Maine. In Florida, a smelly monster called the Skunk Ape was said to lurk in the swampland. Sasquatch sightings also took place in Pennsylvania and other areas of the Midwest. These accounts were accompanied by an outbreak of UFO encounters, so some concluded that Sasquatch was actually an extraterrestrial.

Then, near Greensburg, Pennsylvania, a dozen people said they saw a large red UFO hover above a pasture. They also saw two apelike creatures, standing seven to eight feet tall, slowly walking across the field. When investigators searched the scene the next day, a sulfurous smell permeated the area. One investigator became dizzy and shook violently.

What was behind it all? One theory postulated that electromagnetic energy released by geological stress in the earth played on the brain of the sighters, creating hallucinogenic images of UFOs and Sasquatch in their minds. Another hypothesis suggested that the creatures drew energy from the witnesses. This bloodless vampirism allowed them to emerge into the natural world from another dimension.

CONCLUSIONS ABOUT THESE CREATURES

The debate over Bigfoot, Yeti, and other large furry creatures is still unresolved. Skeptics refuse to accept the few cases of questionable photographs and film footage. And there have been some cases of fraud, where actors roamed about in bulky, fuzzy costumes. Nonbelievers deservedly want a carcass, a skeleton, a skull, or teeth—some kind of physical evidence. If Bigfoot is real, they also ask, then where are the remains of those who died? Disposed of and scattered by scavengers, the believers respond. Besides, the soil of the Pacific Northwest is very acidic and would have dissolved any bones or flesh of a dead monster.

So why not capture or kill one? Those who say they have seen Bigfoot could not bring themselves to shoot it because it seemed so human. In fact, Sasquatch is specifically protected by county ordinances in some jurisdictions. For now, the handful of plaster-cast footprints and scraps of questionable film clips will have to do.

One important argument speaks against the existence of these monsters. There would have to be a considerable number of these creatures available to maintain the gene pool and thus ensure survival of the species.

The essence of this strange search for a hairy monster in our midst is as much a matter of faith as fact, fueled by the argument that detractors simply cannot prove these creatures do *not* exist!

People also claim to see monsters in the seas as well as on land.

Loch Ness Monster

Nestled in the Scottish Highlands, Loch Ness is one of Europe's great lakes. Its length is a modest twenty-four miles, and at most spots it is no more than a mile wide. But its depth—seven hundred feet in places—shrouds it in mystery. Somewhere in that pit a huge monster lurks, or so the story goes.

Legends of monster sightings go back to the sixth century. Early Scots called these creatures water kelpies, water horses, or simply spirits. Mothers warned their children to stay away from the waters. Modern-day Loch Ness sightings began in 1880, when a man examining a sunken boat reported seeing a frightening monster in the murky water. Since then there have been thousands of accounts from the shore and from boats, in the daylight and in the dark. Expeditions costing millions of dollars have taken months as scientists scanned the lake with high-tech equipment. Investigators have launched minisubmarines and probed the depths with sonar equipment. Yet no one has discovered a single bone or other proof of the creature's existence.

A local who aimed his camera at a commotion in the lake first photographed the Loch Ness monster in 1933. A defined, sinuous form appeared on the negative. That photo sparked a Nessie craze. Tourists flocked to the area for a glimpse of the monster. Some who saw it said it resembled a snake or a huge eel. Other said it looked more like a plesiosaur, an aquatic reptile from the age of dinosaurs. Then a surgeon vacationing in the Highlands took the most famous picture. His shot of an animal with an upraised head and neck became known as the Surgeon's Photograph. He claimed it was an undoctored photo, though many experts doubted the claim.

Dozens of photographs and sonar readings later, skeptics still dismiss most of the sightings as mirages, otters, deer, birds, or other conventional animals. They explained the sonar contacts as being caused by boats or stationary objects like tree stumps.

Occult speculation has added to the intrigue about Nessie. One legend tells of a ghost ship spotted sailing through the nighttime waters. In the early 1900s, famed magician Aleister Crowley bought a house near the lake and summoned up demons. His lodgekeeper went mad and tried to kill his wife and children. Soon people began to say that Crowley was conducting human sacrifices to the forces of the Ness. In 1973 that led one clergyman to conduct an exorcism of the lake to banish the evil atmosphere.

More rational explanations of the Loch Ness Monster say that Nessie is an Ice Age remnant of a creature previously thought to be extinct. She might even be a long, serpentine, primitive whale, which evolutionists assumed died out twenty million years ago. Some say she is nothing more than a large seal, whale, or sea cow that wandered in the fresh waters.

Or Nessie might be the monster hundreds of sighters have said she is, an undiscovered species waiting to be revealed when the right camera captures her at the right moment for all the world to see.

OTHER LAKES, OTHER MONSTERS

Though Loch Ness is the most fabled habitat, other large bodies of water have yielded similar tales. Lake Champlain, the long waterway between New York and Vermont, is home to a long-necked creature said to have appeared more than two hundred times. Champ, as he is called, even inspired a New York state resolution to protect him—a move which enticed even more tourists.

Canadian lakes have a tradition of monsters going back for centuries. Lake Okanagan is the site of what Indians called Naitaka, "snake of the water," which was part god and part demon according to legend.

In Sweden, Lake Storsjo has long been associated with monsters. Known as leviathan, the Storsjo monster was said to be white-maned and reddish in color, like an enormous sea-horse.

And in Ireland, many small lakes have their own unidentified inhabitant.

What other aquatic monsters might exist, and what might explain the universality of such speculation? The African python, for example, is large enough to swallow a goat, and has been seen swimming in the Indian Ocean, sometimes traveling from island to island in search of food. Whatever natural explanations might be considered, the evidence that something is swimming, undetected by man, is abundant. Will we ever know the answer? Perhaps more incisive is the question, do we really want an answer?

Unraveling the Mystery

Man craves the companionship of creatures. Witness our national obsession with pets and their care. If some animal is not yet known (especially if its characteristics are nearly human), man's curiosity cannot keep him from trying to uncover the mystery.

God has given man dominion over the earth and the care and control of its creatures. No matter how much atheists deny this implicit impulse for stewardship of all living things, its expression eventually surfaces. I believe the quest to identify aliens of all sorts partly results from this God-given mandate.

Do any creatures like Yeti or Nessie actually exist? I believe they do. Perhaps we will not discover them in the form envisioned by popular myths, but the reports are too voluminous and go back for too many years in a wide variety of cultures to ignore.

Lake monsters could be leftover prehistoric animals, which survived the flood of Genesis. Their adaptability to survive at great depths, and their ability to endure habitats not usually associated with animals of their size, would explain why they have previously been undetected.

And land monsters, like Sasquatch, could also be antediluvian creatures belonging to some subspecies that zoologists have never identified. It is arrogant for researchers to say that everything that can be known about our natural world is now within the grasp of modern science.

What must be avoided is occult speculation that attributes to these creatures some psychic ability to avoid discovery. Equally dangerous is the idea that these beasts are "thought-forms," archetypal images conjured up in the human mind. This theory suggests that humans possess innate extrasensory powers to create mentally what they desire to see.

Clearly, occult curiosity is behind many of the sightings of unidentified creatures. Something in human nature compels humanity to speculate about beings that inhabit the borderland between fact and fantasy. Like our ancestors, who imagined fire-breathing dragons and mermaids, we also invent images of unknown beasts to satisfy our longing for fraternity and mystery. It matters not whether they step off a spaceship or secretly survive in some inhospitable realm. Somehow, somewhere, they are alive, no matter what facts the scientists assemble to disprove their existence. To quote the maxim of the occult television series *The X-Files,* "The truth is out there!"

Unfortunately that truth may be scarier than fiction. The fact is, clandestine creatures do lurk in our midst, and they seek more than to evoke our inquisitiveness—they want our souls!

PART 3

Why Are They Here?

CHAPTER TEN

The Alien Agenda

My personal confrontation with the occult powers behind both witchcraft and UFOs happened during the airing of an *Oprah* television show on which I appeared. I was on the set with an unlikely assortment of guests. Seated to my far right was Laurie Cabot, the official witch of Salem, Massachusetts. To her left, right next to me, was fiction writer Whitley Strieber, author of the book about alien abduction, *Communion*.

Cabot looked like a witch, with dyed coal black hair and a long, flowing black dress and cape. Her eyes were plastered with mascara. On her eyelids she had painted strange black designs that spilled upward into her eyebrows. A half dozen charms and amulets, with occult symbols, dangled around her neck. Every finger of each hand sported one or more rings with odd emblems, tokens of her involvement in the world of magic.

Cabot presented her usual defense of witchcraft. "We believe that God exists in all things, in rocks, and stones, and trees, and within each one of us," she told Oprah. "We practice meditation, healing, and balance, not demons and the devil. We're all part of the god and goddess."

Whitley Strieber was dressed in a conservative gray business suit. With his cropped hair, pallid complexion, and austere glasses he looked like a serious accountant instead of a bestselling author. He smiled politely and answered Oprah's questions about his latest novel.

When my turn came to speak to Oprah, I immediately condemned witchcraft as the work of the devil, clearly denounced in the Bible as an abomination to God.

Strieber instantly ganged up with Cabot to exonerate witchcraft and attack me. When he argued in defense of the occult, I shot back to Oprah, "Read the front page of Strieber's latest book. It's an apologetic for witchcraft. He represents an ideology of Satan that wants people to end up in hell. I want to know what witchcraft has ever done to benefit humanity, like build a hospital."

"Witchcraft can't do that, because it's so small and innocent," Strieber responded with a saccharine sound in his voice that mocked me. "I've learned so much about real reverence from these people, more than I ever learned from my Christian Catholic home. I admire Laurie Cabot because she has the courage to be on this show."

"It's called publicity, not courage," I butted in. "Cabot is here to make witchcraft look good. They need the publicity." I paused. "The real issue is where we're going when we die."

Strieber was furious. He again interrupted me. "Witches are doing something good, something wonderful," he insisted.

"Well, if we're going to talk about religion, let's find out what witches really believe," I said to Oprah. "I want to know what the witchcraft sexual ethic is, I want to know how they deal with the problem of suffering, how they deal with the nature of eternity . . . not all this warm and fuzzy gobbledygook."

"What's your ethic? You tell us first!" Strieber said, running interference for Cabot.

"Read the Ten Commandments," I shot back. "You're the one who is supposed to be a good Catholic. You should know."

"What is it that you have against witches?" Oprah asked me.

"What matters is that there's an eternity, there's a heaven, there's a hell . . ."

"That's what *you* believe," Oprah said, as she challenged me before I finished.

"The Bible teaches in Romans 1:20 that everyone is morally accountable because the nature of God has been revealed through creation . . ."

"That's your interpretation," Oprah insisted. By now I was beginning to feel like it was not just two, but three against one.

"I want to defend Christianity, as a Catholic," Strieber chimed in. "It's getting a bad rap. Christianity is about gentleness and acceptance. It's not about being closed-minded and being afraid of witches!"

Oprah went to a quick break. At that moment, whatever decorum Cabot and Strieber had maintained while the cameras were on was lost. The phony smiles disappeared instantly. Both launched into a verbal attack on me.

Laurie Cabot leaned forward in her chair and fixed her intense, dark eyes on me. She waved her hands furiously. Her long, ratted black hair flew in every direction as she launched into a tirade. "Your bigoted, right-wing brand of fundamental-ism is what burned my ancestors at the stake . . . It's people like you who are the real danger to America. The hate you dish out makes people persecute me just because I'm a witch!"

I glanced at Oprah. Even though she has consistently endorsed New Age practices and has cozied up to the para-normal at every available chance, her church background began to show through. I sensed she felt uncomfortable for me. She stood about thirty feet away with her arms folded, holding her cordless microphone in one hand. She hesitantly took a step toward the stage to intervene, but not in time. Whitley Strieber picked up where Cabot left off.

Strieber's eyes dilated and the veins on his neck stood out. Beads of perspiration formed on his brow. He screamed at me, "How dare you attack Laurie and me. Your (expletive deleted) bigotry is what's really evil. I know that witchcraft is good, and you have no right to say it is satanic."

Unlike many other opponents of Christianity whom I have debated, Strieber could not tolerate any departure from his viewpoint. His rigid body and flinching countenance revealed his utter need for control. Now he became so animated that Oprah headed toward the stage to intervene in what looked like an exchange that might come to blows. Just as Strieber got out of his chair and started toward me, the television floor director signaled the return from the commercial break.

Oprah seemed relieved that she didn't have to intervene since the show was back on the air. Strieber calmed down somewhat but continued to glare at me out the corner of his eye whenever he sensed I was looking his way. What came from his lips, and his spirit, was beyond human indignation.

COMMUNION WITH EXTRATERRESTRIALS

The format of Oprah's show did not permit me to reveal the depth of Strieber's devotion to the occult. I wanted everyone to know that Strieber was an unashamed advocate of the demonic supernatural, and had some strange ideas about extraterrestrials.

Strieber told *People* magazine, "I'm 80 percent sure that [UFOs] are visitors from another aspect of reality, not necessarily from another planet."[1] Strieber's emphatic views have developed a cultlike following. Thousands of people who read his book met in what they called Communion groups to channel spirits and discuss their abduction experiences.

Though he was on *Oprah* to promote one of his other fictional works, Whitley Strieber's real fame has come from his book *Communion*, which describes his alien encounters. He claims that on September 26, 1985, he was awakened in his upstate New York cabin to find a strange being at the bedroom doorway. Strieber says he then blacked out and later found himself in a small room, surrounded by tiny humanoids. One of the creatures inserted a hair-thin needle into his brain, probing and poking. Finally, he was transported back into the bedroom where his wife still slept peacefully.

Afterward, Dr. Donald F. Kline, Director of Research for the New York State Psychiatric Institute, took Strieber through a series of hypnosis sessions, in which he recalled his abduction in lavish detail. Strieber claims that he still gets occasional visits from these unidentified humanoids.

Whom or what did Strieber meet? He isn't sure, but chalks the identity up to "an elaborate encounter with intelligent nonhuman beings . . . goblins or demons or visitors."

Why did it happen? Again Strieber is uncertain. He only knows that "what is happening is that visitors are actually here, or that the human mind is creating something that, incredibly, is close to a physical reality . . . not presently understood by science."

Whom might these visitors be? They are beings with "eyes that seem to stare into the deepest core of being. And those eyes are asking for something, perhaps even demanding it . . . it seems to me that it seeks the very depth of the soul; it seeks communion."[2]

Having faced Strieber eyeball-to-eyeball, I have no doubts about the identity of those beings. Is it coincidental that he so vehemently vindicates witchcraft? Without any intimidation on my part, why was he so enraged by my presence on *Oprah?* His description of being in the presence of extraterrestrials has a fiendish quality. "I felt I was under the exact and detailed control of whomever had me," Strieber wrote in *Communion*.[3] I believe the beings who abducted him were the demons he suggested they might be, and their hatred of God influenced his conduct on the *Oprah* show.

IS THE GOVERNMENT HIDING THE TRUTH?

As you can see, I have reached some very definite conclusions about the aliens Whitley Strieber and hosts of other abductees have encountered. I have also concluded that their intent is evil and their agenda is spiritual deception. But many UFO buffs harbor the notion that our top government officials are the ones with an agenda of deception.

The TV series *Dark Skies* would have us believe that a top-secret government agency known as Majestic 12 (MJ-12) knows all about aliens and is keeping the truth from the American public. I have a copy of the paperwork which purports to be classified material relating to the MJ-12 group, which was supposedly established by executive order of President Harry Truman. These documents claim that

Majestic 12 is a "TOP SECRET Research and Development/Intelligence operation responsible directly and only to the president of the United States." These papers further declare that MJ-12 was formed on September 24, 1947, and includes a list of the scientists and members of the president's cabinet who were the original members.

Under the heading "TOP SECRET/MAJIC EYES ONLY" the report says that in 1947 "four small human-like beings" were discovered "dead and badly decomposed due to the action of predators and exposure to the elements." The bodies were removed for study, the wreckage of the craft was taken to different locations, and "news reporters were given the effective cover story that the object had been a misguided weather research balloon." What was MJ-12's conclusion? They said it is "likely we are dealing with beings from another solar system entirely."

These allegedly top-secret documents relating to MJ-12 have been circulating among UFO researchers since the early eighties. Most of the reputable ufologists have concluded the papers are a forgery or a bit of government disinformation—perhaps to discredit serious UFO research. But the MJ-12 stories have taken on a life of their own, and a growing number of people believe our government is hiding the truth about aliens who have landed in our midst.

Like MJ-12, the reports of alien contacts are sporadic and almost mythic. But the collection of lore surrounding such phenomena is well organized.

Encountering Aliens

Information about alien contact is generally disseminated outside of fourth-estate journalistic channels. For example, underground newsletters notify ufologists of many conventions and other meetings. And a dedicated network of computerphiles and amateur sleuths collect accounts of sightings and abductions on the Internet.

A few hours of browsing the World Wide Web can turn up thousands of UFO sites. The opportunity to exchange such officially ignored information has created a following of cult proportions. That is nothing new to those obsessed with UFOs. Flying saucer cult groups have flourished for decades without the benefit of an interactive computer environment.

Suppose you actually encountered one of these alien creatures? Would you know what to do? You have more options than you might suppose.

For example, you might use your computer to consult a Website known as Schwa. There you will find a company that markets UFO conspiracy theories and actually sells Alien Defense Kits, which include wallet-size alien detector cards.

But real UFO buffs take the idea of aliens much more seriously, and they have actually devised a detailed plan of action. They circulate their warnings and advice in books, self-published newsletters, and on the Internet. Their counsel affirms common sense, but contains a couple of twists aimed at confronting the skeptics. (The inclusion of the following material in this book is not intended as an endorsement of such actions or the organizations recommended. This information is incorporated to show just how serious ufologists are about their pursuit.)

First, if you see a UFO or an alien, hope you have a camera handy. If not, borrow one from the nearest person. The best evidence is a photo taken while the UFO is clearly visible. If you're going to take videos or stills at the moment of the sighting, try to include some other nearby object. That way you'll be able to determine later the relative size of the UFO.

If you have to leave and come back to the scene to take a picture, do it. Photograph any ground disturbances such as a burned landing site or the location of indentations in the ground, which might indicate support pods.

Second, do not wait for the sighting to fade from your memory. Write down everything that happened, what you saw and what you heard, as quickly as possible. Also record your feelings. Did you receive any telepathic impressions? Was your first reaction one of fear, or were you drawn toward the UFO? Make a drawing of your sighting and include as many details as possible. How many lights were there? What color was the illumination? Indicate which direction the UFO was flying and record any abnormalities in its flight pattern.

Third, try to find someone else who can verify what you saw. Scream, if you have to. Make some kind of commotion that will draw a crowd and point them in the direction of your sighting. If there are other witnesses, get them to put their corroboration in writing. The more people who can lay claim to a single sighting, the more credibility you and they will have afterward.

Fourth, don't keep what you saw to yourself. Immediately document what you witnessed by contacting an organization that keeps track of UFOs. The two most prominent are:

The Mutual UFO Network (MUFON)
103 Oldtowne Road
Seguin, TX 78155

Center for UFO Studies
2457 West Peterson Ave.
Chicago, IL 60659

Finally, UFO experts suggest diving into any number of books that speculate, titillate, and inform the reader further about such phenomena. The uninitiated will be shocked to find an extensive library, which runs to nearly a hundred volumes. One warning: Don't expect a scientific approach to the subject. That's too much to ask of this strange matter. Erudite tomes on the topic are few. By the nature of the subject, wild speculation and loosely documented opinions prevail.

Some writers take the agnostic approach—"I'm not sure one way or the other." Their general conclusion is that something is going on, it's mysterious and too frequently reported to ignore, and deserves further investigation. Other authors, like Whitley Strieber, are true believers with an almost evangelistic zeal to win converts to their point of view.

Certain UFO writers are sure they have the answer, and the answer is "No!" These debunkers are convinced the riddle has been solved and propose any number of theories about what UFOs really are. Still others are just as certain they are right, and their answer is "Yes!" They are confident they know who and what is out there and express their ideas with an arrogant naiveté.

If aliens are out there, as some people say, what is their intent for Earth?

The Intent of Aliens

THE STARSEED AGENDA

A series of interesting occult transmissions in the early eighties gave insight into how aliens may be accomplishing their goal. A medium supposedly received channeled communications from extraterrestrials; a collection of these revelations became known as *The Starseed Transmissions*. This medium described an extraterrestrial encounter with identities that were less like individuals; instead they appeared to operate like some kind of galactic organism with specialized informational cells. These "spatial intelligences" went beyond the usual telepathic form of communication to transmit data neurobiologically.

The Starseed aliens also had a way of blending the biogravitational fields of the channeler with their own. The result was a form of direct connection to the human nervous system. Consequently, the channeler simultaneously perceived two realities, his own consciousness and that of the aliens. This synthesis approximated human language and also encompassed a spiritual and emotional understanding, which far surpassed the quality of speech. To those who might worry that this phenomenon was akin to classic forms of spirit possession, the Starseed spokesperson assured the wary that the aliens' purpose was kindly, to teach humanity with angelic intent.

WHO IS IN CONTROL HERE?

Manipulation is the word most often heard by those who speculate about the alien agenda. As evidence, they point to the apparent indifference of aliens to our day-by-day political and social affairs. Our governments and institutions are of no consequence to them, in spite of the often-repeated catch phrase, "Take me to your leader." In fact, no alien encounter I have researched has indicated that any ET has ever asked to talk to the President, Michael Jackson, or even O. J. Simpson. Evidently aliens are not impressed by earthly celebrities or royalty.

Is this manipulation of humanity's consciousness part of an evolutionary process? Some ufologists think so, that man's upward ascent is not the Darwinian product of random selection, arbitrary genetic mutation, and survival of the fittest.

This theory holds that we are being watched over by these aliens, who are carefully conditioning billions of people toward some long-range goal that ignores our daily existence. Some are convinced we are but a step away from learning all about this master plan, that our magnanimous guardians soon will visit Earth to divulge their enigmatic goals.

Several questions about this possibility remain to be answered. Is this majestic design the product of one, or more than one, alien group? Perhaps several sets of extraterrestrials are overseeing the process of man's development, representing some grand council of the universe. Instead of collusion, however, there might be competition. What if rival alien civilizations are vying to control humanity's eventual outcome? And suppose their intents collide and Earth becomes a battleground of opposing evolutionary ideologies? Will earthlings be caught in the crossfire?

Even more bizarre is the conjecture that humanity's development is being assisted by aliens that have assumed biological incarnation. This theory suggests that these entities have in turn produced clones, polluting the human population with humanoid robots, which feed on humans like vampires. Some say they have even entered pets. These aliens may be even more dangerous because they remain undetected by taking on human or animal form.

If this idea of manipulated evolution is a fact, we must also ask when humans became unsolicited participants. Perhaps our biosphere has been the subject of alien interest for thousands of years, and extraterrestrials actually assisted in the building of the pyramids, Stonehenge, and other ancient monuments. Or the intervention may be recent, as part of some countdown to the end of the millennium.

A recurring theme of alien encounters is that they need us,

for some undisclosed reason. Whether they are on assignment to clone our genes, inspect our plant life, or mutilate our animals, there appears to be a motive to their mission. Most ufologists tell us that aliens are spiritually and technologically advanced. So why don't they leave us alone? Haven't they got enough to worry about, running their exalted civilizations?

Maybe the flip of the query is closer to the truth. The consequential question is not why do they need us, but rather, why do we need them?

Do We Need Aliens?

We also seem to need the possibility of other creatures out there for four reasons.

OUR NEED OF ALIENS IS APOCALYPTIC

The obvious reason we need aliens is that the end is near. I'm not talking about true eschatology, which will be covered in chapter twelve. I'm referring to the secular sense of impending apocalypse. From environmentalists to psychic spiritualists, the prediction is the same: As the end of the millennium draws nigh, some end to civilization as we know it is at hand. That hypothesis may have disastrous consequences in dramatic climactic changes. (It may also be more glowing, as the New Age idea that out of Armageddon will come a quantum leap in metaphysical consciousness.)

Historians tell us that as mankind neared the year 1000, doomsday sayers were everywhere, and we can expect them to rise again. This time their most dire warnings are that alien identities lurk on the horizon with disguised intent. Only the vigilant among us will discern their true purposes and survive their invasion.

WE NEED ALIENS TO BE THE BAD GUYS

Every age needs an enemy. The Iron Curtain has fallen. Stalin, Mao, and their successors are dead. Even Castro seems more interested in promoting cigars than exporting revolution. A few Eastern European despots are still around, and Americans seem to ignore the threat posed by the few Islamic extremists in our midst who cry out against the Great Satan of America.

These circumstances are ripe for scapegoating. One reason racism still holds such fascination for some is that it's always easier to blame a distinct social or religious group for a problem, rather than see the more complex vagaries of an issue. Perhaps aliens are now the most exploitable ethnic identity around. They don't look like us, they don't talk like us, and they don't even navigate like us.

Best of all, they aren't from our own planet. And unless we really have a genuine war of the worlds, they can't fight back. We can say what we want to about them in the movies, and they won't send Johnny Cochran to sue us. Their case for cosmic justice will not land at the Supreme Court, and they don't even have a spin-doctor press agent to shape our speculation about their real motives. Millions of light years away, aliens are a safe target.

WE NEED ALIENS TO MIRROR OURSELVES

Perhaps the reason most aliens have some humanoid resemblance has nothing to do with their actual appearance. Though some aliens may really be out there with genuine evil intent, most might be manifestations of the worst we see in ourselves. Is there a connection between the nastiness of our culture and the increasing malevolence of the aliens we encounter on the screen and in real life? If we're frightened that the next aggressive driver will have a gun, or we're concerned that four-letter expletives are the universal adjectives of speech, what do we do? We fight back by projecting our anger about what is distasteful in our midst onto aliens in our galaxy. As Gary Hoppenstand, an associate professor of American thought and language at Michigan State University, put it, "They [aliens] are humans in disguise."[4]

The first of the movies in the series entitled *Aliens,* starring Sigourney Weaver, illustrated such transference. The film depicted the crew of a spaceship as it headed back to Earth from a mission. They encountered a gelid, pulpy mass, which attacked them and lived parasitically off their bodies. This frightening life-form nourished itself until finally destroying its host.

In the film, the creature was eventually ejected from the earthlings' space craft as if it were some organic disease. Thus mankind was saved from this sycophant freeloader, in the decisive way many today would like to be freed from the social cancers of our day.

WE NEED ALIENS TO REFLECT OUR TECHNOLOGY

In our computer-obsessed age, aliens may also be a mirror of our own technological inclinations. Pie-plate saucers will not suffice for today's movies. When George Lucas brought back his *Star Wars* trilogy, even he had to spiff up the images with new state-of-the-art footage. His Industrial Light & Magic facility worked overtime to improve the original movies, including upgraded goo for Jabba the Hut. What we behold in the mirror is a society that demands top-of-the-line tech in every gadget and toy and film. Consequently, the aliens we see in the movies might look like B-grade extras, but they had better have A-grade special effects, which border on the supernatural.

We may need aliens, and they may need us. So what is their ultimate agenda?

The Ultimate Agenda of Aliens

Whether benign and benevolent, or malicious and duplicitous, the intervention of aliens into human affairs clearly serves some purpose. If we reject the evolutionary hypothesis as being contrary to Christianity, then there can be no alien purpose of guarding man's ascension to higher development. What other assumption explains what these beings are up to?

I suspect that the pervasive influence of television and movies, and the milieu of the late twentieth century, have conditioned humanity to an easy acceptance of aliens. Consequently, if a spaceship landed on Earth and stayed around long enough for a photo op, our society would not be overly concerned. After an initial flurry of shock, Americans would quickly go back to their normal routines, sedated by the assumption that what they had long expected had literally come to pass. Once the CNN satellite trucks drove away from the site and the public moved on to the next unusual occurrence, the existence of aliens in our midst would be no big deal. That, more than the prospect of half-human, half-mechanical *Star Trek* Borgs battling the Enterprise, is what is really scary about the agenda of aliens.

I conclude that evil aliens, fallen angelic beings, are clearly orchestrating a social and spiritual mind-set. The irregularity, yet periodicity, of their contact with humans keeps earthlings off balance. We know they have appeared before, and they are likely to appear again, but we can't be certain when it will happen. This creates a neurotic expectation in the human consciousness. The psychological consequence is a mental and spiritual preparation for mankind to welcome, rather than shun, an actual global encounter of the third and fourth kind: contact and communication.

If mankind is indeed being set up for the ultimate deception, then those who are spiritually vulnerable may become victimized by the UFO cults, which are increasing in number and eccentricity as we head toward the next millennium.

CHAPTER ELEVEN

UFO Cults

In 1973 French journalist and race car driver Claude Vorilhon, "Rael" as he is affectionately referred to by his cult followers, said supernatural beings known as the Elohim contacted him. They asked him to be an ambassador to take the final message to humanity and prepare an embassy where extraterrestrials could land. These ETs would bring with them all the prophets of every great religion to usher in the final age of peace and understanding.

Because the word *Elohim* in Genesis means God in the plural sense, Rael concluded that prophets such as Moses, Buddha, Muhammad, Joseph Smith, and others were all part of the same godhead. Together they deliberately chose one among themselves to deliver the proper message to each age. Jesus Christ's task was to spread the message to prepare for this critical "Age of Revelation." In this era, the advances of science would finally allow us to understand the Elohim purpose of loving all humans as the children of these extraterrestrial gods.

I confronted Rael on my radio talk show and quickly discovered that UFO cult leaders like him have insulated themselves from any objective inquiries. In spite of the fact that Rael espoused the illegitimate bearing of babies, cohabitation with alien beings, and the sexual exploitation of children, he seemed unmoved by any attempt to suggest that his ideas were an immoral abomination.

I want to warn you there are more dangerous groups like Heaven's Gate and these UFO groups are not to be taken lightly. They are a hazardous addition to our cultural climate, which already fosters many dangerous religious cults.

The Raelian Cult

Devout Raelians wear large medallions with a swastika inside the star of David, which they believe is an ancient symbol of time and space. Members participate in four annual festivals, usually marked by nudity, so that the Elohim can fly overhead and register the Raelians' DNA code on their UFO machines. New initiates sign a contract that permits a mortician to cut out a piece of bone in their foreheads, where the psychic third eye resides, after death. This bone is then stored in ice awaiting the descent of the Elohim.

New members must also send a letter of apostasy to the church where they were baptized. Above the ordinary Raelians is another class of the cult known as the "Structure." These more devoted followers of Vorilhon must be committed to building an embassy in Jerusalem by the year 2025 to receive the extraterrestrials.

Although the Bible is quoted at length in cult materials, Rael makes it plain that Scripture contains only traces of the truth. He believes that the occult Jewish Cabala is the richest of all divine testimonies.

Using the parts of the Bible that fit his thesis and discarding the rest of Scripture as "poetic babblings," Rael teaches his followers that alien scientist-creators scouted Earth as a place where they would create life-forms. The tree of the knowledge of good and evil in the Garden was actually the scientific books by which these aliens accomplished their goal. The serpent was a symbol of a group of scientists who wanted mankind to have the knowledge forbidden to them by these aliens.

RAEL AND THE BIBLE

Rael puts his own extraterrestrial spin on nearly every major biblical incident. The flood, for example, occurred when aliens in a spacecraft nuked the planet, which resulted in a tidal wave that destroyed all life. The tower of Babel was an enormous space rocket. The parting of the Red Sea took place by means of a repulsion beam from a UFO.

On Mount Sinai, it was aliens in a spaceship, not God, who visited with Moses. The walls of Jericho fell down because of complicated alien instruments that emitted supersonic waves. Samson's long hair was a form of telepathic antennas, which communicated with his alien creators. The Ark of the Covenant contained an atomic-powered cell, which transmitted and received messages from these space beings; the horns of the altar were actually levers for this transmitter-receiver. Such disingenuous explanations are just an example of Rael's strange theology.

To continue with Rael's overview of the Old Testament, the fourth man in the fiery furnace, who saved Shadrach, Meshach, and Abednego, was one of these aliens. The chariot in which Elijah was taken to heaven was actually a spaceship, and Jonah's whale was really a submarine.

Rael's interpretation of the New Testament is just as absurd. The three wise men were guided to Bethlehem by a UFO, he says. At the proper time, these alien creators revealed their true identity to Jesus and taught him scientific techniques, which the people of his time perceived as miracles. When Christ walked on water it was by means of an anti-gravitation beam. When he rose from the dead it was through resuscitation by these friendly extraterrestrials.

Moving beyond the gospels, Rael says that the tongues of fire in chapter two of Acts were a visible display of amplified telepathic waves, which imprinted the minds of the disciples with other languages to spread the truth of God.

For those seeking the comfort of an afterlife, Rael assures followers that upon death every particle of one's body is capable of re-creation. A grand council of eternal aliens assembles to judge whether those who lived on Earth are worthy of another life. There is hope that after death the sincere seeker of these aliens will be scientifically reincarnated on a planet of "eternals" to live forever. On the other hand, those who don't heed the message of these aliens may suffer the destruction of a "final furnace."

RAEL AND SEX

Contemporary topics are also very much on Rael's mind, and many of them center on sex. He openly teaches that sex with anyone at any time is acceptable, especially if one's partner is of the same sex. He also encourages group sex. The only rule is that all participants be in agreement with the behavior. This leads to a teaching he calls "sensual meditation," which is usually done with a partner of the same sex as a means of reaching "the sublimation of harmony which enables you to approach infinity." Critics charge that the public nudity associated with Raelian gatherings is further evidence that Rael has fostered a sex cult under the guise of extraterrestrial interest.

Rael's ideology of sex is rooted in his teaching that he is only passing on the customs of space aliens. These creatures took him to their planet, where he observed a society of ninety thousand quasi-immortal men and women who had united themselves and thus eliminated all forms of jealousy. Consequently, Raelians are encouraged to seek a "cosmic orgasm." They are also told that genetic engineering through eugenics is possible by psychic control during intercourse.

Rael discourages marriage and discounts long-term relationships. "When you no longer get on well together, do not remain together," says Rael. He lauds sexually active single mothers, and if they no longer desire the children they bore, they are given permission to dump them. "If a child becomes a nuisance, entrust him to society," Rael explains.

Beyond Rael's endorsement of homosexuality and bisexuality, is his approval of trisexuality and even quadrasexuality. The latter is reserved for those who seek sex with the Elohim, to achieve extraterrestrial ecstasy. It's little wonder that strippers, transvestites, and aggressive homosexuals are part of the Raelian cult. After all, when the UFOs descend, sexual deviancy will be the path to salvation.

What about suicide? Everyone has a right to it. Active euthanasia? No problem, Rael says. Necromancy? Telepathic communication with the dead is both sanctioned and encouraged. The ultimate thread holding all these perverse beliefs together is the message that the Elohim aliens, as the creators of man, must be loved and welcomed when they arrive on Earth. For now, one must telepathically seek to receive the love they beam down.

Since its heady days of the 1980s, the Raelian UFO cult has suffered from several bizarre incidents, including murder. In Quebec, Canada, where Rael has a large following, a member of the cult was sentenced to six and one-half years in jail for the manslaughter of a fellow member. The killer, Orville Frenette, who believes Claude Vorilhon is the messiah of this age sent to welcome aliens to Earth, underwent a court-ordered mental examination. A psychiatrist testified that Frenette believed he had done the will of God when he mutilated the other cult member.

THE RAELIAN REVOLUTION REVEALED

At the height of Raelian popularity, my radio talk show featured one of the cult's representatives, Michael Beluet, from Montreal, Canada. Beluet's conversation was so preoccupied with promoting the licentious sexuality of Raelians that it was no shock when he admitted that Raelians teach that parents should "show children how to get pleasure from sex."

Michael explained that he was one of ten people who had organized five thousand Canadian followers. He personally described sensual meditation as a way to connect with infinity by being more aware of the senses. He also actively promoted abortion, mercy killing, and homosexuality. Michael quoted John 16:13 ("However, when He, the Spirit of truth, has come, He will guide you into all truth") to proclaim that Rael is the extraterrestrial equivalent of the Holy Spirit.

A woman named Donna, a follower of Rael, called the show to proclaim her devotion to the Elohim. She had been a Christian missionary for three years and had memorized over two thousand Scriptures from the Bible. Donna now said she believed that the Virgin Mary was artificially inseminated by an extraterrestrial. Rael had given her the answers she never found in church.

Another caller named Charles also said he came from a Christian background. He insisted that he searched the Scriptures diligently and could find no reason to reject the teachings of Rael. A lady named Mary Ellen said she had followed Rael for ten years. A surgeon who performed delicate operations to cure myopia called long-distance from France to affirm his faith in Rael.

RAEL ON THE LINE

Finally, Rael himself called from France. He claimed that he was half human and half alien, and explained, "My father was from the planet of Eternal Life in our galaxy. He was also the father of Jesus. My mother was impregnated while on a UFO, but the memory of exactly what happened was taken from her."

Just when I thought Rael had said the most preposterous thing possible, he would make an even more outlandish statement. He told me the Elohim said that life on Earth is not the result of random evolution but deliberate creation. An advanced race of people manipulated DNA to make humans "in their image. The Bible account of creation is just one of several religious texts describing this event," he explained. "All religious books refer to this same act."

"What gives you the right to reinterpret almost everything in the Bible?" I wanted to know.

"I speak directly from the mouth of the people who gave the Bible to human beings in the first place, the Elohim," Rael answered. "The Old Testament is a true book, but the New Testament is 95 percent wrong. Hitler was the Antichrist, and the time of the Bible is finished. We are now in the golden age of love and fraternity."

My years of experience interviewing the most difficult of guests was no help. I could not connect Rael to reality. His mind was quite literally in another world, and no matter what I said he did not deviate from his demented beliefs. He espoused his views of free sex and veiled pedophilia, to say nothing of his claim of being an alien half-breed, with a calmness that was frightening. I concluded that he was either a marvelous actor or truly deranged.

Unfortunately the Raelians are just one of many UFO cults. Let me guide you through a labyrinth of cults and cult teachings, which demonstrate our current captivation with UFO phenomena. This brief historical analysis should serve to illustrate how humanity has been gradually conditioned by aliens of some sort to accept the idea of extraterrestrials spiritually intervening in the affairs of earthlings.

UFO Cults

You might be surprised to find out that UFO cults began as long ago as 1758, when Emanuel Swedenborg published *Arcana Coelestria: The Earths in the Universe.*

THE SWEDENBORGIAN CONNECTION

Emanuel Swedenborg was born the son of a pious, eighteenth-century Lutheran minister. He became a dynamic intellectual and a member of the Swedish Diet. His expertise in the fields of metallurgy and crystallography led him to travel widely, but at the age of fifty-two he answered what he felt was a divine call to become a revelator of the symbolic meanings of Scripture.

The philosophy of what became known as Swedenborgianism taught that those who die enter an intermediate state where they prepare for heaven or hell. In hell, a person becomes an evil spirit, but in heaven a person attains angelic status. In this life after death, each soul retains the physical appearance of early adulthood as it was lived on Earth.

Swedenborg became involved in practices of spiritualism such as automatic writing and astral projection. During these journeys to the spirit world, he communicated with what he believed were angels, who convinced him that the Bible needed special interpretation. In *Arcana Coelestria: The Earths in the Universe* Swedenborg claimed that his out-of-body travels had taken him to various planets and even beyond our solar system. He revealed a detailed portrait of life on Mars, including particulars of Martian anatomy. Unlike the popular novels of his age which chronicled voyages of fantasy, such as *Gulliver's Travels*, Swedenborg's treatise claimed he had actually journeyed to outer space.

Swedenborg's writings introduced to later centuries the idea of beings on other planets who were superior to earthlings. The inhabitants of Mars were loving and peaceful, he said, devoid of the competitive greed found on Earth. Interestingly enough, Swedenborg was only able to visit planets that were known to exist at that time, so there is no reference to journeys to Uranus, Neptune, or Pluto in his work. But in the starry realms Swedenborg did visit, he encountered such ascended inhabitants as St. Augustine and even the apostle Paul.

In the nineteenth century, an even greater variety of spiritualists followed in Swedenborg's tradition.

SWEDENBORG'S DISCIPLES

In the 1890s, a French medium named Helene Smith said she had traveled to Mars, and offered drawings of the animal and plant life she saw there. She even spoke and wrote a language she claimed to have learned on the Red Planet. Critics today note, however, that Smith reported at length on Martian canals, a popular "discovery" of that era. Smith's American contemporary, Sara Weiss, also drew on popular scientific assumptions to promote her ideas of Martian life.[1]

The psychic explorers of the nineteenth century were the forerunners of today's UFO abductees. Since these alien investigators lived in an age before manned flight, their journeys were usually by means of astral projection, generally during a séance. These trips to alien environments provided a rationale for discarding traditional biblical teachings in favor of occult doctrines, supposedly taught by spiritually ascended extraterrestrials.

What these nineteenth-century (and earlier) ruminations about alien life-forms have in common with today's abductee accounts is a remarkable confirmation of common inspiration. For example, in the book *The Gods Have Landed,* religious cult expert J. Gordon Melton notes that pre-twentieth-century alien contacts were established by psychic/occult means. The idea of telepathic communication with alien life-forms was also an 1880s idea. Melton observed, "Contactee accounts emphasize the message, which is usually metaphysical. The information concerning the planet (being psychically visited) serves merely to authenticate the lesson to be learned." Melton further notes that the Martians contacted by one nineteenth-century psychic conveniently verified a major spiritualist doctrine.[2]

The cult of Theosophy raised this endorsement of the occult to an even higher level.

THE THEOSOPHICAL CONNECTION

Helena Petrovna Blavatsky, born in 1831 of an aristocratic Russian family, exhibited psychic tendencies at an early age. As an adult she explored Hinduism and other forms of Eastern mysticism, which were popular intellectual pursuits of that age. She claimed that during her travels to Tibet she made contact with disembodied higher spiritual beings, whom she called *mahatmas*. Along with two other prominent occultists of her time, Colonel Henry Steel Olcott and William Quan Judge, Blavatsky formed the Theosophical Society in 1875.

The key to Theosophy's appeal was its slight departure from spiritualism. According to Blavatsky, spiritualists only contacted the lower levels of psychic entities. She was more concerned with receiving directives from the ruling masters of the spirit world: various Buddhas, ascended masters, and one supreme deity known as the Lord of this World.

The extraterrestrial key to Blavatsky's cosmology was the notion that Venus was the residence of her alien masters. The Venusian lords had the Lords of the Seven Rays under them, extraterrestrial beings who communicated directly with spiritualist mediums such as Blavatsky. This relationship between mortals and highly evolved aliens was the precursor of today's cinematic portrayals from *E.T.—the Extraterrestrial* to *Close Encounters of the Third Kind*.

THE GUY BALLARD CONNECTION

In 1930 an occultist named G. W. (Guy) Ballard claimed he was visited by St. Germain, a spiritual being who had attained "Christhood" during his time on Earth. Under the pen name Godfre Ray King, Ballard published two books extolling his relationships with the ascended masters. Ballard declared the existence of a cosmic government whose hierarchy consisted of former earthly residents. Through the teachings of these revered discarnate entities, each person could recognize the I AM presence of God within.

Ballard said he was in contact with aliens from Venus, who were similar to Blavatsky's Lords of the Seven Rays. This time around, the extraterrestrials called themselves the

Venusian Lords of the Flame. Though nineteenth-century occultists had flirted with the idea of human-to-alien associations, it was Ballard who truly began building a religion based on extraterrestrial communication.

Ballard believed in being a regular contactee of his alien lords, and these messages formed the doctrines of his religious system. Thus the modern contactee movement was born. The main tenet of Ballard's sect was that increased spiritual consciousness, under the tutelage of these otherworldly masters, would lead the way to a new interplanetary dimension of universal cosmic understanding. The message of these aliens from six decades ago sounds very much like the current metaphysical messages from UFO occupants: World destruction is imminent without the help of ascended aliens who offer hope from the "octave of life," which will, if heeded, solve all the world's problems.

The present-day Elizabeth Clare Prophet cult, The Church Universal and Triumphant, is the spiritual stepchild of Guy Ballard's teachings about an elevated spirit plane of alien ascended masters of the Great White Brotherhood. This mysterious cult, now headquartered at Royal Teton Ranch in Montana, has drawn much media attention because of its apocalyptic mentality, which warns of a coming nuclear holocaust.

One of the best known and longest lasting UFO groups is the Aetherius Society, founded in London in 1956 by Dr. George King.

THE AETHERIUS SOCIETY

An openly metaphysical group, the Aetherius Society encourages members to be willing channels of communication for extraterrestrial beings. Dr. King's involvement in spiritualism and various forms of occultism suited him for leadership of this strange cult. King said he received a message from the "cosmic brotherhood of space masters" in May 1954. That first message was explicit: "Prepare yourself! You are to become the Voice of an Interplanetary Parliament."[3]

The cosmic brotherhood chose King to be the chief "Primary Terrestrial Mental Channel" of a 3,500-year-old being named Master Aetherius from the planet Venus. Aetherius, whose name means "one who comes from outer space," and a spiritual leader called Master Jesus asked King to wage war on the side of certain "space masters" who battled "black magicians" living on Earth. King claimed more than six hundred extraterrestrial communications, which he called "transmissions."

To receive these transmissions, King went into a trance state to contact a supposed higher psychic center. Then the masters channeled a telepathic beam of thought through him, which localized in his voice box and emerged in perfect English. These channeling activities were more frequent when one of Master Aetherius's spaceships was orbiting Earth and sending out special power—bursts of cosmic psychic energy known as "pushes."

Many of Aetherius's messages warned about the use of nuclear energy and called for a return to cosmic law as taught by Jesus, Buddha, and Krishna. These spiritual leaders were said to have come from other planets, which were free from war and disease. Inhabitants of these planets explored the galaxies at will. When they visited Earth, it was to participate in psychic adventures aboard what are seen as flying saucers. The goal of these visitations was to monitor our planet to ensure the survival of the human species.

The most important date on the calendar of the Aetherius Society is July 8, which commemorates the visit of a gigantic spaceship in 1964. At that time the craft manipulated the Earth's cosmic energies. All these activities, as described by King, proceed from an Interplanetary Parliament headquartered on Saturn. The society also teaches that Lemuria and Atlantis were two previous civilizations on Earth, which perished due to atomic warfare. The cosmic masters communicating through the Aetherius Society are bent on preventing that from happening again.

Reincarnation is part of the Society's beliefs, including the idea that the current human race came from another planet in this solar system. That original home was destroyed by an atomic explosion and mankind was reincarnated on Earth eighteen million years ago. The future goals of the Aetherius Society include an extraterrestrial Second Coming, when an outer space Master will arrive on a flying saucer to offer people on Earth a choice: either learn the cosmic laws of the New Age, or be destroyed and eventually reincarnated on another planet. As an alternative, Society members predict that Christians could look forward to eventually joining Jesus and several Christian saints for an eternity on the planet Venus.

The Society, currently headquartered in Hollywood, California, claims to have a collection of UFO gear, including a radionics device and a plexiglass pyramid "energy radiator." Members of the Society claim that their prayers to the plexiglass have actually averted "the big one," the earthquake that would have thrust southern California into the sea.

Several years ago I personally interviewed the United States representative of the Aetherius Society, Dr. Alan Mosely, on my nationally syndicated talk show.

AETHERIUS ON-THE-AIR

Mosely, a doctor of divinity and self-proclaimed instructor of yoga and the "psychic sciences," spent more than twenty years in the Society. As to the entities that used Dr. King as a channel, Mosely declared, "We know that these intelligences pilot what we call flying saucers. They've been here for thousands of years and the job of the Society is to put forward their teachings."

He further explained that the cult had expanded into a congregation of Aetherius churches with prayer services to "God." These churches, Mosely declared, also practiced the laying-on-of-hands for spiritual healing. He compared the Second Coming of Christ to an invasion of friendly aliens, saying, "When you look at the references in the Bible to the glory of the Son of Man coming on great clouds with power, what are you talking about? A cloud of power is a spaceship. After all, the first sightings of UFOs were several hundred thousand years ago, recorded in the Hindu scriptures."

When I asked him if King's transmissions heralded a coming world savior, Mosely answered, "We've been told that when the messiah will come, the world will know, and there won't be any question. It won't be Jesus. Don't get me wrong, I have a profound love for Jesus, who is an aspect of God, but then all of us have an aspect of the divine in us."

As Mosely explained the essence of the Society's teachings, he described how King would go into a yogic trance to experience the "bliss of God." Then he would telepathically contact "cosmic masters, individuals who have gone further on the road of evolution . . . They don't die."

"Exactly who are these beings?" I asked.

"One was a being known as Jesus," Mosely replied. "He said, 'Blessed are they who work for peace, blessed are they who love. The workers for peace are thrice blessed because they sacrifice their own joy.'"

At the time I wondered why anyone had fallen for King's cosmic con job, transmitting higher truth that had already been spoken in the Beatitudes of Matthew's gospel, chapter five. Obviously King's followers had not bothered to read the Bible.

Mosely also identified several other beings, one a being known as "Mars Sector Six" who orbited the Earth, and had journeyed "quite possibly from Mars."

Many cult organizations, like the Aetherius Society, start their own religion by eclectically taking bits and pieces from all spiritual traditions. Another UFO organization that does so is the Deist Research Institute.

DEIST RESEARCH INSTITUTE

The Deist Research Institute (DRI) combines the idea of extraterrestrials with the Bible. According to DRI literature, UFOs are piloted by a race that understands "time dilation" and thus are not bound by space and time limitations. Rather than traveling from other planets, they emanate from a huge mother ship that revolves around the Earth. According to DRI beliefs, the New Jerusalem spoken of in Scripture (Revelation 21:2) is a veiled reference to this huge spaceship. Since time is meaningless to the mother ship occupants, there is an unlimited opportunity to study humans on Earth.

The Institute theorizes that space beings are interested in mapping the genetic code of humans and animals. Since mankind on Earth was supposedly created by using DNA from various species of beings, one can only guess what other kinds of races may be on the drawing board.

According to DRI literature, man ended up on Earth as a result of his spiritual retrogression, "the fall." The fall of man in the Garden of Eden was a test, a necessary evil. The serpent was not at fault but the buck was passed to him so that Eve could avoid her own responsibility. In fact the devil, the serpent, was not evil at all, but merely became a scapegoat for man's lack of accountability.

Flying saucers? These are "gyros," personal recreational aircraft of the time-dilation creatures. Gyro pilots even formed groups, and they have choreographed spectacular sky shows with their sophisticated lighting systems. The gyros are powered by a nuclear fusion engine, which makes no noise and is one cubit in diameter.

The Deist Research Institute believes, like Scientologists, that man was once a god, but unfortunately, man has genetically retrogressed to become mortal. As a hybrid race, half-god/half-human, man evolved to his current state of mortality through ignorance. DRI members believe that the only hope of recovering Eden lies with the unidentified aliens patiently circling the Earth.

UNARIUS FOUNDATION

San Diego is home to the Unarius (**UN**iversal **AR**ticulate **I**nterdimensional **U**nderstanding of **S**cience) Foundation, started by the late Ruth Norman, a self-described cosmic visionary. Norman, who also went by her space name, Uriel, claimed to have received transmissions from supercelestial beings and to have traveled by astral projection to more than sixty planets. Like many New Age channelers, Norman said earthbound beings could reach a higher spiritual plane by heeding the communication of extraterrestrials. Her goal was to prepare a welcoming committee of devoted earthlings to greet thirty-three starships of the Interplanetary Confederation when they land in San Diego in the year 2001.

Norman got her start in the world of UFOs in 1954 when she met her husband, Ernest, at a psychic convention. He gave mediumistic readings and had been involved with several spiritualist churches. He told Ruth that in a past reincarnation she had been the daughter of the pharaoh who raised Moses.

The Unarius cult really took off when Ernest was supposedly contacted by extraterrestrials and channeled their messages. The Normans published a set of books, called the *Pulse of Creation* series, which contained clairvoyantly transmitted communications from beings on Mars and Venus. These ascended spiritual masters said they were using the Normans to send previously unrevealed knowledge to Earth. The masters claimed to possess infinite intelligence, which could be understood by tuning into vibrational energies. Doing so would allow cult members to heal themselves and to travel astrally to the universities of other planets for instruction in the ways of the masters.

After Ernest's death, Ruth's channeled messages increased until she began to view scenes from the planet Eros. Eventually she claimed she was engaged to the archangel Michael, and was crowned Uriel, Queen of the Archangels. The occasion was marked with an earthly reenactment of the astral wedding ceremony. Further messages from beyond included the wisdom of everyone from Plato to Socrates, plus the channeled voice of John F. Kennedy. After that, other extraterrestrials from more than thirty planets delivered a series of messages over several years.

Along with seven of her pupils, Norman placed a four thousand-dollar bet with England's biggest bookmaker, Ladbroke & Co., on 100 to 1 odds that space aliens would land in the year 1975. Her students also pooled their money to raise another fifteen hundred dollars for the bet. Norman claimed she got the information by "mental attunement" with extraterrestrials.

As a promotional gimmick for her cult, the wager went well. But when 1975 came and passed Norman had to adjust her prophecy. Yet this failed prediction had little effect on her credibility with devoted followers.

She next claimed a revelation that the Intergalactic Confederation would converge on Earth in the year 2001. Huge flying saucers, Norman said, some as big as five miles in diameter, would land one on top of the other in the Bermuda Triangle. They would discover the lost library of Atlantis, and humanity would learn how to solve all its economic and social problems. Work would cease and all peoples would serve each other. Knowledge would increase by the wearing of a cap, which would enable a person to read a book every night.

But that's not all! A series of Power Towers, consisting of high-tech mirrors, would meet all the planet's energy needs. The Space Brothers from the UFOs, powerful spiritual healers, would train earthlings in ways to achieve global peace. All who would come in contact with these Brothers would have their consciousness raised to a higher frequency so they could experience the love of these aliens.

Elderly and bedridden, Ruth Norman died in 1993 at age ninety-two after informing her followers that the Space Brothers had given her permission to leave her body. According to the reading of her will, she promised to return in 2001 with the Brothers. She also pledged that, upon her return, she would pick up her Space Cadillac, an early 1970s model with a tiny flying saucer on the roof. Unarius groups still meet, mainly to hold classes that explore past lives on other planets. Art therapy is part of the curriculum, a talent said to come from the "transceived" wisdom of higher intelligences.

Charles Spiegel, 76, retired psychology professor at San Diego State, now heads the organization which has adopted the more official-sounding name, the Unarius Academy of Science, now headquartered in El Cajon, California. Their immediate goal is to prepare for the year 2001, when Unarius members believe a UFO from the planet Myton will land in the Bermuda Triangle on a submerged, but soon-to-rise, land mass that once was home to the mythical lost city of Atlantis. Spiegel explains that the Myton landing will be beamed to the entire Earth on TV. Of the Mytons' intention, he says, "These are humans like us, but highly evolved. They come as consultants, like the Peace Corps, to help us join with the thirty-three other Earth-like planets.[4]

THE CULT LIST IS GROWING

Every day some new group springs up somewhere, while other cults are discredited or disbanded. As we approach the year 2000, we can expect cults with UFO-centered beliefs to proliferate.

For example, extraterrestrials told the Solar Light Center, headed by Marianne Francis, that man is presently living at the end of a twenty-six-thousand-year cycle and that light energies are seeking to cleanse the Earth. This cleansing will be the Second Coming of Christ, the dawning of a golden age ushered in by extraterrestrials. To prepare for this apocalyptic event, cult members seek to telepathically channel intelligences from outer space. The Center borrows the often-used metaphysical concept of a Great White Brotherhood and believes that eternal truths have been given by all great spiritual avatars, including Jesus, Buddha, and Krishna.

There has even been one alien-sponsored candidate for President of the United States. In 1960 and again in 1972, a man named Gabriel Green ran for president because he said aliens told him to do so. Green, founder-president of the California-based Amalgamated Flying Saucer Clubs of

America, Incorporated, said he personally met with friendly extraterrestrials and still maintains telepathic links with them. When they might encourage him to throw his hat in the political ring again has not been revealed.

Conclusions About the Cults

UFO cults are some of the most bizarre aberrant groups on America's religious landscape. While their focus is on alien encounters, their teachings suggest a tragically misled search for spiritual meaning. The almost total unaccountability of their leaders results in astonishing excesses as well as incredible claims. Yet notable similarities bind these disparate groups to a single inspiration, which is opposed to a biblical interpretation of morality and reality.

FIRST SIMILARITY: LEADERSHIP

Nearly all UFO cults are headed by a single charismatic figure. While that characteristic is true of most non-UFO cults as well, the UFO groups assign their leader a unique status. It is one thing for the head of a cult to espouse an unusual interpretation of the Bible or some sacred book. It is quite another thing for that person to receive direct revelation from an extraterrestrial source. Who can argue with someone who says that Jesus and other past spiritual adepts speak through their bodies or telepathically communicate with their minds? Followers can only conclude that the claims are legitimate, or that the leader is fraudulent or psychotic—and then face the disapproval of the group.

SECOND SIMILARITY: SPACE BEINGS

The beings whom the cult leader has contacted are always wiser and more benevolent than earthlings. Invariably, they are preparing humanity for some event of cosmic significance. These beings give deference to Christ or whatever religious figure has been previously dominant in the minds of cult members. Often their message is one of impending earthly doom unless their guidance is heeded. If their message is obeyed, however, cult members are promised personal serenity and peace on Earth.

THIRD SIMILARITY: ESCAPISM

An element of escapism pervades most UFO cults. Such avoidance may be mentally possible through astral projection to other worlds. It can also be acquired by an emotional denial of temporal realities in favor of a cosmic interpretation of life's difficulties. Sometimes this escapism is quite literal. A spaceship is soon to land and, like the angelic craft of *Close Encounters of the Third Kind,* it will spirit away the chosen ones. Cult members must serve the group to prove their worthiness for a compliant abduction when the aliens arrive.

FOURTH SIMILARITY: SPIRITUAL EVOLUTION

In UFO cults, the problems of humanity are never attributed to a sinful, fallen nature, which is the traditional Judeo-Christian explanation. Beings on Earth are seldom ascribed negative attributes of greed, jealously, and lust, which would hinder brotherhood and compassion. Instead, the true predicament of humanity is said to be a lack of spiritual evolution. This shortcoming is always contrasted with the higher state of advancement attained by the space aliens, who want to coax humanity upward to a more lofty state of spiritual understanding.

FIFTH SIMILARITY: AN AMORAL UNIVERSE

The message of these advanced, compassionate extraterrestrials is curiously devoid of any objective moral criterion.

There are no "thou shalt nots" on other planets. No Ten Commandments guide their conduct. Our space brothers are beyond that. Instead, alien-influenced leaders ask us to shed most inhibitions. Doing so, they say, allows cult members to tap into a universal intelligence that is beyond dos and don'ts. Once we acquire this higher consciousness, it will supposedly guide our actions on Earth toward humanity's eventual sexual and spiritual liberation on other planets in the next life.

This overview of quirky cult teachings about UFOs and aliens shows that for over two hundred years the doctrines of a new religion have been forming. But does the Bible endorse this alien-based apocalyptic worldview? Will extraterrestrials really be involved in God's end-time program? Will Christians be raptured, lifted off the planet, by UFOs? Or has some dark force simply been preparing people to accept that explanation? These are the questions I will answer next.

CHAPTER TWELVE

ETs
and
the
End Times

Sitting in front of a microphone, where every weekday afternoon I broadcast my live, nationally syndicated radio program, is always an experience with an adrenaline rush. Live radio is risky. You never know what a caller is going to say, and my right index finger is rarely more than an inch or two away from the "Profanity" button. We broadcast with a three-second delay, so anything that is unsuitable for airing can be deleted with one deft flick of my finger.

A few months ago I readied myself to hit this button for different reasons. This time I considered bleeping out the guest I was interviewing, not because her words were off-color, but because they were outlandish and bordered on blasphemy. I continually confronted her illusions so my audience would see the error of her incredible beliefs.

"You say that God, or Yahweh, as you prefer to call him, was the leader of an alien contingency that visited Earth on UFOs and used advanced technology in his dealings with man, right?"

"That's correct," my guest, Ann Madden Jones, author of *The Yahweh Encounters: Bible Astronauts, Ark Radiations, and Temple Electronics,* replied.

"You also claim that Mt. Sinai was a UFO landing port, that the tabernacle in the wilderness was a microwave transmitter-receiver for space-to-Earth communications, and that the purpose of the blood on the altar in the tabernacle was to ground electrons to facilitate this transmission. That's not only blasphemous, that's downright weird!"

"I do get some reactions like yours," my guest responded, "but most of the reactions have been very affirmative."

I took a deep breath. I was not only outraged at the sacrilegious claims of Ann Madden Jones, I was also somewhat nonplussed by the ludicrous basis for her assertions.

But I soon learned that what I'd already heard was only a small sample of her atrocious beliefs. I regretted that she was talking to me by telephone, so I was not able to look into her eyes, which I suspected must have had a very strange gaze.

From the cover copy of her book I read: "The Holy Bible reveals an unsuspected panorama of events in ancient history which range from interplanetary space travel, human genetic engineering, Earth orbit communications, thought control, sonic holography, crystal lasers, resurrection by bioelectrical patterns, and human cloning."

Laying Ann's book on the counter in front of my broadcast board, I leaned closer to my microphone. "Let me be sure I get this right. Are you saying that the supernatural phenomena we read about in Scripture are the manifestation of UFOs?"

"Yes," Ann replied, "but these aren't my ideas. They're

based on what the Bible says from Genesis to Revelation. Read it without a religious point of view, look at it technologically, and it's hard not to come out with my conclusions that Jesus was an alien in contact with God by means of a mindbeam."

I took another deep breath and again felt the urge to hit the "Profanity" button. This conversation was truly being launched into the ozone.

"Are you claiming God is in a spaceship?"

"Yes. Read Exodus 24, it's all there."

"If you're right about this God-alien stuff, why didn't the Almighty just say so plainly?"

Ann explained her thesis. "Just like UFOs today are very elusive, they were the same in the Old Testament. That's why the prophets' actions were puzzling to the writers of the Bible."

I was so frustrated by this part of the interview that I insisted Ann state her basic hypothesis as simply as possible before going further.

"Here's what I believe," she said. "The Jews were a chosen race, born of extraterrestrial seed. When Moses got the Ten Commandments, God landed on Mt. Sinai in a spaceship; that's why there was fire and smoke everywhere. That's also why the children of Israel had to send out a scapegoat. It was not an offering for sin, it was a way of testing the radiation levels from UFOs that landed periodically."

"You're serious?"

"Very much so. You see, God was in a spaceship, hovering above the tabernacle. He communicated to the priests by means of special microwave receivers in the clothes they were wearing. There were crystals in the ephod of the priestly garments to demodulate the messages of God."

"Why didn't God tell people what He was doing?" I insisted.

"How could He? They wouldn't have understood what was going on back then."

"Ann, I can hardly understand it today!"

By this point in the interview I decided it was time for me to take over and put some perspective on what Ann was saying. I politely asked her to wait a moment while I set forth my side of her story.

"God doesn't need to excuse what He does and how He does it," I countered. "He doesn't need to obfuscate His intentions because we're incapable of understanding what He wants to tell us.

"This is a typical tactic of esoteric cults. They claim that the truth of God must be secretly interpreted, and that the Bible does not really mean what it appears to obviously say. Instead it must be properly deciphered by someone with cryptic understanding of Scripture's hidden truths."

I went on. "In Matthew 18:3 Christ said, 'Unless you are converted and become as little children, you will by no means enter the kingdom of heaven.' If God intended *children* to understand His message of love and reconciliation, He would not have hidden it in language with a double meaning about aliens and spaceships."

Ann's occult interpretation of the Bible was what really bothered me, so I zeroed in on that. "Was Jesus the Son of God?" I demanded to know.

"Yes, He was."

"You mean the extraterrestrial son of God."

"However, you want to look at it," Ann said. "He was the only begotten Son of God, according to the Bible."

"What about the Virgin Birth?"

"Well, you must understand that when I say Jesus was born

as the Son of God I look at it a little differently. God was a superior advanced being who came here in a spaceship. They called him the 'Living God' in the Old Testament. Today we'd call him a living alien astronaut. He had the capacity to beget children by Earth women. Mary's conception by the Holy Spirit meant her bearing the child of this alien God."

"You've just discounted the third person of the Holy Trinity!"

"No, when the Holy Ghost fell on people and they spoke in tongues, it was an information transfer from God in his spaceship."

"Wait a minute! Do you claim to be a Christian?"

"Yes," Ann responded. "If by that question you're asking if I believe Jesus is God, the answer is yes. But I also believe Jesus is a half-breed, part human and part space alien."

By this point in our conversation I could hardly wait to see what she thought about the End Times. I thumbed through her book and came upon a partial explanation: "When the Bible talks about a new heaven it means the Earth has acquired a new orbit around the Sun and a different orientation to the stars. John in his Revelation saw the ultimate interplanetary mother ship, the headquarters of Yahweh called the New Jerusalem."

I turned to my guest. "What I read here in your book is that the city foursquare, the eternal destiny of the saints of God, is in fact a flying saucer."

"Yes, after all the disasters of the apocalypse, the mother ship will come to Earth. That's what John saw descending."

"Ann," I argued, "how is there going to be room on a spaceship for millions of Christians?"

"The Bible says we'll go to heaven in a changed form. Maybe that means only our genetic blueprint will be resurrected, not our physical bodies. You could have a lot of those in a space-ship and then duplicate them later from the DNA of a single cell."

As Ann's ideas became more and more bizarre I wanted to know what had led her to speak out on such weird notions. "Ann, you've got a B.A. in psychology, and you've been a school teacher," I said. "What in the world motivated you to spend fourteen years writing a four-hundred-page book argu-ing that God is an ET?"

"When I lived in Florida, before I started writing the book, I had an encounter with an invisible force," she answered. "It was a frightening experience, and when it was over I knew I was going to write a book about God and UFOs."

"Can you be more specific about this experience?"

"Sure," Ann said. "I was all alone in my house. I was feel-ing fine, and there was nothing strange going on, when sud-denly I felt a presence. I thought it was a burglar at first. I tried to get up from my chair and couldn't. Finally I tried to lunge from the chair, but when I stood I was knocked down on the floor by some force. I was terrified. I remembered there was a gun in the master bedroom and I decided to get it. I crawled down the hallway toward the bedroom when I realized it was foolish to counter an invisible force with a gun. I saw the Bible laying on a table beside the bed and wrapped my arms around it. I prayed, 'Whoever you are, just tell me what you want and what you want me to do!'"

Ann paused for a moment. It was obviously an emotional moment for her to remember such terror.

"Did you ever find out what was happening, and who was doing it?" I asked.

"Eventually, whoever was overwhelming me put the

thoughts into my mind," Ann said reverently. "I had to write a book, and it, or they, or whoever, was going to help me do it.

"After that, I had no choice. I had to read stuff on UFOs. An obsession came over me to find out about extraterrestrials. I had no control over it and couldn't stop until I finished."

"How do you know if it was good or evil?"

Ann's answer was disturbing. "I don't know. But I don't see how it could be evil if the Bible has all this stuff in it about UFOs, and I've just discovered it. It must be the truth, and people have to know it. Anyway, if it's not good, the truth will eventually come out."

MY ANALYSIS OF ANN

Notice how Ann's introduction to the idea of extraterrestrial communication meshes with other accounts you have read in this book. I have researched hundreds of abduction accounts and stories of alien encounters, and almost universally the victims felt panic and terror.

The next emotional response, as it was in Ann's case, is a feeling that the alien being exercises complete control. The contactee's life purposes become subservient to the goals of the extraterrestrial, and they may decide, as Ann did, to be a missionary of the aliens' message.

Ironically, most who claim alien contact accept their lot with the same resignation as Ann did. It's as if the contactee's soul has been so invaded, the person realizes that struggling against the extraterrestrial's will is futile. Like Ann they ignore the warning signs of an evil takeover.

Ann's beliefs illustrate the aliens' agenda to discredit the Bible. First, they question the accuracy of the Old Testament by saying that the prophets who wrote the Bible were ignorant of God's true purposes. If these men of God could not properly explain the appearance of a spaceship on Mt. Sinai, how can they be trusted to communicate the essence of salvation? If the scapegoat of sin had no relevance to forgiving transgressions, and if the blood on the mercy seat was not there for an atoning purpose, everything else Scripture says is suspect.

If the miracles of God can be explained away as examples of extraterrestrial intervention, all awe of God's power is gone. If God is merely an exalted space being, and Jesus no more than a highly evolved half-breed, then any idea of Christ's crucifixion as the pivotal point of history is meaningless.

Most importantly, the blessed hope of all Christians—that we shall know eternal bliss with Christ in His heavenly glory—is destroyed. If the New Jerusalem is an oversized aircraft, then the majesty of living there with God eternally is a matter of technological marvel, not an inexplicable wonder.

And if the anticipation of resurrection is an ethereal event in which our identity is no more than DNA imprint, any aspiration to be in the presence of Christ is meaningless. Plainly put, the alien message of extinguishing our personality in exchange for a ride on a spaceship erodes the concept of being in the presence of Christ at His Second Coming to experience "joy" and "rejoicing" (1 Thess. 2:19).

It should be obvious by now that some sinister force is deliberately developing a religious system in preparation for spiritual world domination. With equal amounts of spiritualism, ascended-masters teachings, Theosophical thought, and occult orientation, a Mystery Babylon belief is slowly creeping into modern consciousness. For more than two hundred years the momentum has been building to establish a creedal structure that includes a confirmed set of doctrines, disciples, apostles, and supernatural validation.

The doctrines are the messages of alien abductors. The disciples are those who look to UFOs as the hope of humanity.

The apostles are the abductees who have had direct contact with alien benefactors. The supernatural validation is the consistent accounts of UFO sightings and close encounters.

I have already explained how the message of UFO occupants meshes with the New Age and other occult philosophies surrounding the paranormal. Ann's episode has particular relevance in showing the eschatological motif.

ETs at the End of the Age

In addition to endorsing psychic phenomena and occult supernaturalism, extraterrestrials seem concerned about getting their message out at this particular time in human history. Much of their emphasis is on events related to what the Bible calls "the great tribulation" (Rev. 7:14).

The return of Jesus Christ at the end of time has been the focus of serious theological speculation and fanciful cultural conjecture for nearly two thousand years. Preachers throughout the ages have consistently warned that Christ's discourse on the Mount of Olives cautioned against setting a time too specifically. "But of that day and hour no one knows, not even the angels in heaven, nor the Son, but only the Father," Jesus said (Mark 13:32).

Yet we are also told that Satan has some indication of that hour. While the devil's knowledge of this timing is not exact, it is close enough to solicit his fury "because he knows that he has a short time" (Rev. 12:12) to accomplish his last intentions. It is therefore reasonable to assume that the devil has enough inkling to begin preparing for the war of the ages (Rev. 12:7).

In recent history it seems that Satan has been more aggressively setting the stage for the Antichrist's takeover of Earth.

The appearances of UFOs and the message of aliens dovetail perfectly with this scheme.

And, believe it or not, some so-called Christians try to fit the idea of UFOs into their biblical worldview, just as Ann did.

CHRISTIAN UFOLOGISTS?

Salvation, for these unorthodox believers, is reaching the kingdom of God by a mass alien abduction. They teach that heaven is an actual locale, just outside the Earth's atmosphere. They believe that the catching away of the devout, as described in 1 Corinthians 15:51–52, will be accomplished *Star Trek* style. The "saved" will be beamed up by a flying saucer and transported to a higher level of the resurrected saints.

Christian ufologists see flying saucers as one of the signs of heaven described in Matthew 24. Space creatures are angelic agents of God who have been brought here from their homes in other parts of the galaxy. All biblical revelations are the result of UFO interventions, and today's extraterrestrial contacts are a form of continuing prophecy and divine revelation. Like my talkshow guest Ann Madden Jones, Christian ufologists consider the supernatural to really be the supertechnological.

Before reaching final conclusions about the purpose of UFOs in the age leading to Christ's coming, let's look at what we have determined so far.

A POSSIBLE CONCLUSION

First, a large body of evidence supports the thesis that something is going on out there. Some UFOs are real and their existence has an empirical scientific explanation, which may not be in the realm of current knowledge.

Second, discounting the cases that science can (or will

soon) decipher, other UFO phenomena cannot now, and will never be, explained by natural theses. These UFOs appear to be a spiritual or nonmaterial curiosity, which warrants serious consideration by those who hold to the Christian faith.

Third, after decades of considering the conspiracy theories, there is not sufficient proof to conclude that UFOs are man-made. If some government or human agency on Earth is behind it all, surely the proof would have leaked out by now. If such advanced technology were in human hands, greed for control or financial gain would have caused someone to attempt to use such exotic techniques.

Fourth, while the Bible does not explicitly rule out extraterrestrial life-forms, there is sufficient scriptural evidence that life on Earth was created by God as a special act of divine grace, duplicated nowhere else in the universe. Thus the aliens who contact us cannot be from another planet or solar system.

Having eliminated all natural explanations for the strange occurrences surrounding the flying-saucer phenomenon, one must conclude that the source of UFOs is extradimensional. Such appearances do not have the attributes associated with godly angels, so there must be another supernatural derivation.

Biblical logic then concludes that demons, fallen angels, are the creatures behind legitimate UFO occurrences. In a major book about UFOs, a New Mexico medical doctor claimed to have encountered Grays who told him, "We occupy all space . . . everywhere in the universe or any void between. We are from a different dimension, a different plane of existence. We have no boundaries or limits. We are an antilog of everything you see visually. We can travel in any dimension and occupy the same area as say, Earth, but not the same time or space without being observed."[1]

Isn't this the way a demon would describe his characteristics and abilities? The material phenomena associated with UFO sightings must be some kind of matter/energy manipulation understood by the archenemy of God. The forces of darkness must have understood the theory of relativity, $E=mc^2$, which explains the interchangeability of energy and matter, long before Einstein stumbled upon its secrets. Thus the UFO occupants are demons, and their craft some sort of materialized energy.

Christians who analyze the UFO phenomenon take into consideration more than the apparent hostility of some aliens, as reported by certain contactees and abductees. Believers look for signs that are consistent with the Bible's warnings about the spiritual deception of "doctrines of demons" (1 Tim. 4:1). As I have repeatedly shown throughout this book, and in my conversation with Ann Madden Jones, the message of extraterrestrials is obviously intended to lead people away from an orthodox interpretation of Scripture. In the broad sense, this is the work of the antichrist spirit, because it denies that Jesus is the only true Lord incarnated in human flesh (1 John 4:1–3).

But does the appearance of UFOs herald the coming of *the* Antichrist?

The Ultimate Invasion

Until recently any talk of demons in a prophetic context was considered cause for a visit to a psychiatrist. Both subjects, evil spirits and an apocalypse, were equally taboo. No more. The novels of Stephen King and the movies of Clive

Barker have popularized the concept of evil's embodiment. Likewise, society seems consumed with a feeling that some kind of imminent Armageddon awaits humanity. Today, even those who do not hold to a high view of Scripture are curious about good and evil angels, as well as cataclysmic events leading to some kind of final spiritual confrontation.

Since the time of Jesus, when His disciples wanted to know what signs would herald the "end of the age" (Matt. 24:3), Christians have also been curious about the Second Coming of Christ. Such anticipation is well justified. Followers of Jesus are encouraged to look forward to the "blessed hope and glorious appearing of our great God and Savior Jesus Christ" (Titus 2:13).

In popular Christian parlance, this event is known as the Rapture. While that particular word is not used in Scripture, the concept of a supernatural "catching away" of Christians is taught. An angelic summons, complete with the sound of a trumpet, is spoken of in 1 Corinthians 15:15–52. Then, the dead in Christ will first be raised and, immediately afterward, those remaining alive on Earth will be "changed" (they will be supernaturally transformed into immortal beings).

There is reasonable biblical evidence that this Rapture will involve some kind of rising from the ground into the atmosphere. Matthew 24:30–31 speaks of Christ returning in the clouds above the Earth. (This passage also reiterates the sounding of a trumpet and the calling together of God's people from every corner of the globe.) In 1 Thessalonians 4:16–17 the apostle Paul specifically states that those Christians who are alive at the time of Christ's return will respond not only to the angel's trumpet, but they will also be beckoned by the personal invitation of Christ ("the Lord

Himself will descend from heaven with a shout . . ."). Then they will be "caught up" (raptured) to meet Jesus.

What relevance does this have to the issue of UFOs? First, notice that the accounts of alien abduction, many of which have been cited in this book, contain descriptions of being snatched away into the air. In some cases the abductees felt they were somehow dematerialized and beamed up. In other instances they were bodily sucked upward into a hovering flying saucer. Is this similarity of description merely a coincidence, or are alien abductors really evil angels conducting some kind of mock dress rehearsal to counterfeit the miracle of the Rapture of God's saints?

What purpose would this serve? Christians who adopt what is known as a premillennial interpretation of Scripture believe that the Rapture will occur approximately three and one-half years before the Antichrist comes to power. In fact, the ability of the Antichrist to deceive those on Earth will be the direct result of almost all Christian influence having been removed from this planet. But how will this instantaneous disappearance of millions of people be explained?

If the popular novels and nonfiction books churned out by Christian prophecy experts are correct, the immediate earthly consequences of the Rapture will be disastrous. Christians in airplane cockpits, behind the wheels of automobiles, and wherever they are in control of equipment or machinery, will suddenly disappear. The carnage and destruction will be unlike any natural disaster this world has ever experienced. To restore order on Earth, an answer will be needed.

What if the Antichrist, or his precursors, were to suggest that benevolent beings from beyond had actually done those remaining on Earth a favor, by a mass abduction of Bible-believers? After all, hadn't the devout followers of Christ been an irritant? Weren't people on Earth sick of the Christian opposition to abortion, same-sex marriage, assisted suicide, and a host of other "socially progressive" measures? With these interfering meddlers out of the way, a quantum leap in spiritual understanding would at last be possible, without narrow-minded fundamentalist bigots standing in the way, finding evil in every new approach to the paranormal or the occult.

Granted, the immediate consequences in death and suffering as the result of this benevolent human hijacking would be devastating, but the long-range result would be a spiritual enlightenment of far greater significance. In fact, the Christians could be blamed for the suffering caused by the abduction. After all, the necessity of removing them from Earth brought on the catastrophe. The horror caused by the disappearance of Christians would be a small price for earthlings to pay for being able to institute a worldwide religion, founded on an ecumenical blend of Eastern mysticism and secular humanism!

John's Revelation makes it clear that the time of the Antichrist's reign will be an era of intense spiritual activity. It won't be godly religion, but it will be religion. Revelation 17 shows that the whoredom of the End Times will be a devout system of false spirituality, most likely an amalgam of occult and heretical teachings. The religion of UFO occupants and abductees certainly qualifies as a strong candidate.

Consider this scenario. After decades of conditioning, a UFO actually lands and beings disembark. Instead of looking repulsively reptilian, they assume a more humanoid appearance, like the Nordics or blond Venusians I described earlier. They claim to be superior beings from both a militaristic and intellectual standpoint. However, they offer to come in peace if humanity will accept their ideas of spirituality, which promise to save the Earth from impending doom.

As proof of their more advanced powers, they perform great wonders in front of the world's television cameras. These aliens are able to evoke life from inanimate objects, as a precursor to the apparent miracle of Revelation 13:15 ("He was granted power to give breath to the image of the beast . . .") Among their signs is the awe-inspiring sight of fire falling from heaven (Rev. 13:13). After decades of sci-fi conditioning, humanity would accept such paranormal feats as the highly developed abilities of these supercreatures.

These beings would attract two elements of society. On one hand they would appeal to the New Age mentality, which thirsts for demonstrations of nonrational psychic activity. At the same time, secularists and atheists could easily accept the feats of these beings as having some natural explanation because of their more advanced technological acumen. With New Agers and secularists on their side, aliens could supplant the Christian view of history as the testimony of a personal God's intervention to reconcile man to Himself by the Cross. In its place would be a syncretistic dogma that suggests the "salvation" of humanity is in the hands of a superrace, which has interceded to rescue earthlings from their worst urges.

How should the people of God respond to the present assault by evil aliens? What is the best defense against their demonic deception?

THE CHRISTIAN COUNTERATTACK

First of all, Christians must have a solid foundation in biblical doctrines. Second, we must become acutely aware of this overwhelming assault on the Christian worldview.

While many moms and dads probably pay little attention to the current UFO craze, their children and grandchildren most likely do. The movies and television programs mentioned in this book cannot be dismissed as benign entertainment, or just the latest Hollywood fad.

The possibility exists that these media influences will seriously alter a young person's spiritual outlook. Parents need to explain that movies like the *Star Wars* trilogy were deliberately concocted with a mystical view of reality, and that concepts like "The Force" are based on metaphysical interpretations of good and evil, and are therefore anti-biblical.

A teenager might even read a book by Ann Madden Jones, or some other alien advocate, or hear one of them interviewed on television. Parents must make sure their children know the Bible, so they can test these beliefs against Scripture.

Parents must also make their children aware of the dangers surrounding occult curiosity. The paranormal must be off-limits, no exceptions. Explaining the difference between the supernatural power of God and the demonism behind occult feats will remove the fascination some children might have for such acts.

As more and more messages are received from extraterrestrials, and as these communications are dispersed in the entertainment media, and even the news media, the likelihood increases that remaining aloof from such doctrines of demons will be almost impossible for anyone living in our culture.

A friend at church or one of your neighbors may be duped by books or television interviews about UFOs. Christians need to be biblically grounded and know what God's Word says about the issues addressed in this book, such as life on other planets, evolution, psychic supernaturalism, and the scriptural view of life in these Last Days. We need to listen to our friends and neighbors to help them sort through these confusing ideas to find the truth.

Looking back over the many examples of UFO sightings I have given, I feel compelled to caution, "You haven't seen anything yet!"

As we draw nearer to the Rapture, the diabolic "signs and wonders" that Jesus warned might deceive some Christians (Matt. 24:24) will likely intensify in frequency and awesomeness. After all, once the aliens have conditioned us to accept extraterrestrial intruders, there will be no reason for these invaders to hold back.

Remember that Pharaoh's magicians, described in Exodus 7–8, performed amazing feats, including turning water into blood and rods into serpents. In these Last Days we should expect no less from so-called extraterrestrials. As a result, there can be no substitute for constant vigilance in the face of this evil alien invasion.

God is not in a spaceship. Exodus 24 does not say this. And Jesus is not a half-breed alien. He is the unique God-man, and the *only* name by which we can be saved (Acts 4:12).

Do not let your loved ones or friends forfeit their salvation by accepting the false doctrines preached by aliens. The Lord is counting on us to denounce the demonic activities of these Latter Days.

The truth which many elitist UFO groups, including Heaven's Gate, have focused on is that the gate to eternal life is indeed narrow and "there are few who find it" (Matt. 7:14). But in the very next statement Jesus warned, "Beware of false prophets" (v.15). How then may one avoid the errors of paranoid and suicidal cults and know which voices are those of fraudulent spiritual leaders?

A little further in Matthew 7 Christ explained, "Whoever hears these sayings of Mine, and does them, I will liken him to a wise man who built his house on the rock" (v. 24). The prudent seeker of truth is one who carefully studies the sayings of Jesus found in the Bible and consults a variety of wise, mature, theologically qualified Christian counselors. Then he is able to build his spiritual house astutely on a solid foundation. The ultimate error is to pursue the gate of an alien agenda instead of seeking the Gatekeeper who is the Way, the Truth, and the Life.

NOTES

Chapter 1   *Heaven's Gate or Hell's Door?*

1. "Out of This World," *Time,* 20 October 1975, 25.
2. "Bo-Peep's Flock," *Newsweek,* 20 October 1975, 32.
3. Elizabeth Gleick, "The Marker We've Been Waiting For," *Time,* 7 April 1997, 42.
4. James S. Phelan, "Looking for: The Next World," *New York Times,* 29 February 1976, 12.
5. Ibid., 64.
6. Ibid., 57.
7. "Californian Found Dead in Cult Copycat Suicide," Associated Press report, *Denver Post,* 2 April 1997, 10A.

Chapter 2   *The Alien Invasion*

1. "Millionaire buys Utah ranch for its UFO appeal," *Arizona Republic,* 27 October 1996, A15.
2. Robert Macy, "Road paved with close encounters," *USA Today,* 19 February 1996, 8A.
3. Ibid.
4. Alex Jack, "The Air Force smoke screen," *East–West Journal,* February 1979, 12.
5. Ibid., 13.
6. Lisa Faye Kaplan, "Too-close encounters," *USA Today*, 16 December 1993, 11A.
7. Richard Corliss, "A Star Trek into the X-Files," *Time,* 7 April 1997, 42.
8. Ibid.
9. Ibid.

Chapter 3   *Is There Really Life on Mars?*

1. Adam Rogers, "Come in Mars," *Newsweek,* 19 August 1996, 56-58.
2. Leon Jaroff, "Life on Mars," *Time,* 19 August 1996, 58-65.
3. John Noble Wilford, "New Traces of Past Life on Mars," *New York Times,* 11 November 1996, A6.
4. Paul Hoversten, "Clinton pledges search for proof," *USA Today*, 8 August 1996, 1A.
5. Jaroff, "Life on Mars," 62.
6. Terence Monmaney, "Just how earth-shaking is life-on-Mars discovery?" *Los Angeles Times* report, *Denver Post,* 2 September 1996, 2A.

7. Ibid.
8. Ibid.
9. Rogers, "Come in Mars," 61.
10. Jaroff, "Life on Mars," 62.
11. Hollis Engley, "Chances are somebody's out there," *USA Today,* 16 December 1993, 11A.
12. Paul Hoversten, "Jupiter moon may support life," *USA Today,* 14 August 1996, 11A.
13. Kavita Varma, "Planet has potential for water, life," *USA Today,* 18 January 1996.

Chapter 4   *UFOs and Hollywood Hype*

1. "Steven Spielberg's Musings on Poltergeist," *People,* 11 November 1982, 62.
2. Rick Marin, "Alien Invasion," *Newsweek,* 8 July 1996, 50.
3. *USA Today,* 10 July 1996, 10A.

Chapter 5   *New Age Nuttiness and Psychic Phenomena*

1. Marin, "Alien Invasion," 52.

Chapter 6   *Seeking Extraterrestrial Signals*

1. Paul Hoversten, "NASA searching for cosmic feedback," *USA Today,* 24 February 1989, 3A.
2. Ibid.
3. Jaroff, "Life on Mars," 64.
4. Ibid.
5. "Star Talk Without Oprah," *People,* 16 November 1992, 19.
6. Jacques Vallee, *Revelations* (New York, N.Y.: Ballantine Books, 1991), 290.
7. Maria Goodavage, "Circles in the fields inspire talk of UFOs," *USA Today,* 15 November 1990, 6A.
8. "Around and Around in Circles," *Time,* 18 September 1989, 50.
9. "It Happens in the Best Circles," *Time,* 23 September 1991, 59.
10. "Duo flattens theories on crop circles," *Rocky Mountain News,* 10 September 1991, 3.

Chapter 7   *Aliens Among Us: Abductions and Walk-ins*

1. Marie Brenner, "East Side Alien," *Vanity Fair,* March 1990, 175.
2. Gene Emery, "When they come, he'll be ready," *Washington Times National Weekly Edition,* 29 May–4 June 1995. Emphasis added.
3. Ibid.
4. Ibid.

5. Mark Shaffer, "A trucker vanishes, and UFO believers are abuzz," *Denver Post,* 4 August 1996, 10A.

6. Ibid., 11A.

7. Frank Huznik, "Carried Away?" *USA Weekend,* 23–25 June 1993, 4–6.

Chapter 8   **UFOs and Evil Aliens**

1. "Tracking the Cattle Mutilators," *Newsweek,* 21 January 1980, 16.

2. "Cow suffers weird death on ranch." This article was cut out of a newspaper, and I am not sure of the reference.

3. Joanne Ramondt, "Mutilations grip Alberta's attention," *Calgary Herald,* 13 October 1979, A2.

4. Linda Moulton Howe, *A Strange Harvest,* KMGH-TV, 1 April 1983.

5. Howe, *An Alien Harvest* (Cheyenne, Wyo.: Pioneer Printing, 1989), 57.

Chapter 9   **The Alien Index**

1. Joe Lewels, Ph.D., "The Reptilians: Humanity's Historical Link to the Serpent Race," *Fate*, June 1996, 44-52.

2. *Mysteries of the Unknown,* (Time-Life Books, 1988), 106.

Chapter 10   **The Alien Agenda**

1. *People,* 11 May 1987, 39.

2. Whitley Strieber, *Communion* (New York, Avon Books, 1987), 3–5.

3. Ibid., 15.

4. Susan Wloszczyna, "Space invaders infiltrate films," *USA Today,* 27 September 1996, 2D.

Chapter 11   **UFO Cults**

1. James R. Lewis, editor, *The Gods Have Landed* (Albany, N.Y.: State University of New York Press, 1995), 4.

2. Ibid., 50.

3. Ronald D. Story, editor, *The Encyclopedia of UFOs* (Garden City, N.Y.: Dolphin Books, 1980).

4. Paul Hoversten, "With 2000 near, UFO believers taking off," *USA Today,* 31 March 1997, 2A.

Chapter 12   **ETs and the End Times**

1. Lewis, *The Gods Have Landed.*

ABOUT THE AUTHOR

Bob Larson is an expert on cults, the occult, and supernatural phenomena. He is the host of a daily one-hour radio show, "Talk-Back with Bob Larson," heard in approximately 150 cities in the United States and Canada, and host of a weekly television show. He has lectured in more than seventy countries and has appeared on such television shows as *Oprah, Donahue, Montel, Sally Jesse,* and *Larry King Live*.

Larson is the author of twenty-five books, including the novels *Dead Air, Abaddon,* and *The Senator's Agenda*, as well as *In the Name of Satan, Satanism: The Seduction of America's Youth, Straight Answers on the New Age,* and *Larson's New Book of Cults*.

Other books
by Bob Larson

Straight Answers On the New Age

This comprehensive Christian look at the New Age Movement stands as the definitive reference work for clergy and laity who need to know the potential dangers of these radical beliefs. Answers to commonly asked questions follow each topical overview along with a quick and easy index of people, places and terms associated with the subject.

0-8407-3032-2 • Paperback • 288 pages

In the Name of Satan

In this book about defeating the forces of evil, Bob Larson dispels the myths surrounding Satan and his demons, providing readers with the knowledge that they need to withstand the devil and discover a victorious God. *In the Name of Satan* shows you what you can do to prevent Satan from taking control of your life, and the lives of others around you.

0-7852-7881-8 • Paperback • 240 pages

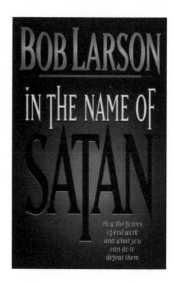